J. Summerland

JUNIOR JETSETTERS™ guide to VANCOUVER

Junior Jetsetters™ Guide to Vancouver
First edition 2010
ISBN-13: 978-0-9784601-5-0

Published in Toronto by Junior Jetsetters Publishing, a division of Junior Jetsetters Inc.
3044 Bloor St. W., Suite 550, Toronto, ON M8X 2Y8 (Canada)
Text: Pedro F. Marcelino, Slawko Waschuk
Sub-Editor: Anna Humphrey
Characters: Tapan Gandhi
Illustrations: Ran Kim
Cover Design: Pedro F. Marcelino, set in Casual Font by A.J. Palmer
Cover Art: Ran Kim, Tapan Gandhi (logo), Kim Sokol (stamp).

Special Thanks to: Lida Bucyk, Caren Austin, Ken Medoro, Carol Gomez, Lydia Miller.

Library and Archives Canada Cataloguing in Publication

Marcelino, Pedro F., 1978-
    Junior Jetsetters guide to Vancouver / Pedro F. Marcelino, Slawko Waschuk ; edited by Anna Humphrey ; illustrated by Tapan Gandhi and Ran Kim.

ISBN 978-0-9784601-5-0

    1. Vancouver (B.C.)--Guidebooks--Juvenile literature.
I. Waschuk, Slawko, 1974- II. Humphrey, Anna, 1979- III. Gandhi, Tapan, 1986- IV. Kim, Ran, 1984- V. Junior Jetsetters VI. Title. VII. Title: Guide to Vancouver.

FC3847.18.M37 2009   j917.11'33045   C2009-904249-5

Printed and bound in China by Everbest Printing Co Ltd.

activitiEs iN vaNCouvER

YOUR list of stuff to SEE and do

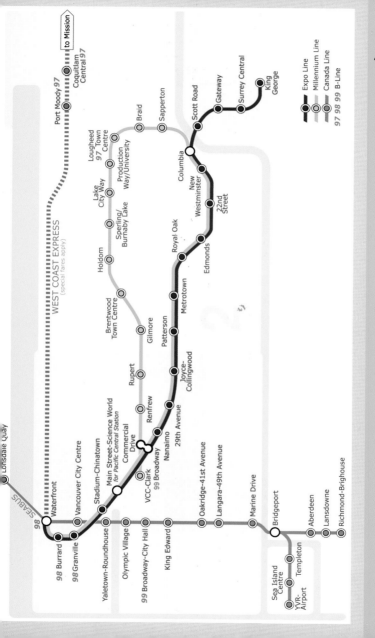

wHat do you KNoW about VaNCouvER?

Vancouver is the largest city in British Columbia, although it isn't the province's capital city (Victoria, on Vancouver Island, is). This coastal city is a popular place for nature lovers, with the ocean, rivers, bays, beaches, forests, and mountains all within a few minutes from downtown. It's a modern city deeply connected to the outdoors and the environment, and all of its natural features help make it one of the nicest-looking places to live in the whole world.

HoW cool iS tHat?

Vancouver, the 'Gateway to the Pacific', has been known by several names. Its location at the end of the Canadian Pacific Railway earned it the nickname Terminal City. Early Chinese called it Saltwater City. Today, you might hear people call it Vancity (which is also the name of its biggest credit union). The city is also often called Hollywood North, because of the many films produced here.

Water is one of the highlights of Vancouver, and you can't really get away from it. Thousands of people flock to the countless beaches every night to watch the sunset. Right by the beaches, the Seawall (a path for pedestrians, cyclists, and rollerbladers) extends about 20 kilometres around the city, most of it right by the waterfront. Vancouver's urban layout and all the water surrounding it fostered a unique architectural and city-planning style, now known internationally by the word 'Vancouverism'.

a liTtlE HistoRy

tHE FiRst NatioNs pEoplE Got tHERE...wEll...fiRst

About 10,000 years ago, the glaciers from the last ice age began to disappear from the area we now know as British Columbia. Eventually, people moved to this land. These Indigenous peoples of the Pacific Northwest Coast are known as the Coast Salish. The Coast Salish were not one group, but were made up of many bands and nations, living throughout British Columbia.

Vancouver is located in the territory that was once occupied by three First Nations peoples: *Sk̲wx̲wú7mesh* (Squamish), *Tsleil-Waututh* (Burrard or 'People of the Inlet'), and *X*ʷ*məθkʷi?əm* or *Xwméthkwyiem* (Musqueam). It was an ideal place to live, and to gather food and materials. Villages and settlements were located all over the area, including in today's Stanley Park, Kitsilano, and North Vancouver.

captaiN vaNcouvER sailEd iN

The first Europeans to explore the area arrived by ship. Spanish Captain José María Narváez explored the Strait of Georgia in 1791. A year later, a British Captain named George Vancouver, who decided to expand on the Pacific exploration of James Cook, met up with another Spanish expedition, and together continued to explore the Strait of Georgia. The Spanish Banks, a beach near the University of British Columbia, was named to commemorate this meeting.

CITY OF VANCOUVER

Captain Vancouver surveyed the area in small boats and arrived at present-day Vancouver before the Spanish. He named the spot where he landed Point Grey, and the water around it Burrard Inlet.

NEW GERMS and NEW RULES WERE dEVEStatiNG FoR tHE iNdiGENOUS pEoplE

The arrival of the first Europeans had a pretty major impact on the Indigenous peoples. The Europeans brought with them diseases to which the Indigenous people had never been exposed, and their communities were soon devastated. Years later, when the government instituted a policy of assimilation (which meant that the Europeans made the First Nations people gradually adapt to their own customs and start using English, a European language), the local population and culture again declined dramatically.

tHE HudsoN's bay compaNy Got iNto tHE FuRRy busiNESS

Around the same time Captain Vancouver was surveying the area by sea, explorers were making their way west by land from Upper and Lower Canada in the east. The first to arrive was Simon Fraser in 1808. The final leg of his journey was along a river, now named after him. Simon Fraser was a fur trader who worked for the North West Company of Montréal. In 1821, that company merged with another trading company named the Hudson's Bay Company. This new company, which continued to be known as the Hudson's Bay Company, now had a huge, and exclusive, trading territory. At that time, the border between the British and the Americans had not been established. In order to protect as much territory as possible from the Americans, the Hudson's Bay Company built a trading post on the south side of the Fraser River. This post was named Fort Langley.

PEOPLE MADE THEIR FORTUNES FROM GOLD, THEN WOOD!

In the 1850s, gold was discovered in California. This was the start of a gold rush that eventually reached Fort Langley and helped shape the history of (the future) Canada. The area became the Crown Colony of British Columbia. The gold rush passed and soon lumbering became a major industry on the coast and along Burrard Inlet. Sawmills were built and before long timber was being exported from the area.

THE Railway Rolled into town

Meanwhile, on the other side of the continent, the eastern British colonies confederated and became Canada. They convinced British Columbia to join them, in return promising to build a railway that would connect the new province to the east. In 1867, near a lone lumber mill, a saloon opened and soon the entire area became known as Gastown, after the saloon owner, John 'Gassy Jack' Deighton. Gastown was to be the end of the new railway, and, in 1886, was incorporated as the City of Vancouver. The area had grown over the previous 20 years, and consisted of about 400 buildings. Shortly after, the Great Vancouver Fire hit and all but two of the buildings were destroyed. However, the city was rebuilt and the first train arrived from the east. Vancouver grew quickly, thanks to the railway and the new port. Tourists could now travel from the east, and the resources of the west coast could easily be transported either to the east on the railway or overseas through the port.

11

PEoplE camE FRom NEaR and FaR

During the 20th century, Vancouver continued to grow. The city became home to people of all ethnic backgrounds from all over the world. Many Chinese came to Canada to build the railway, most of whom remained and settled near the coast. Chinatown prospered. Many Japanese came to British Columbia to settle and became successful fishermen and gardeners. The city was also home to many Indians, primarily Sikhs, who came from India, another British colony.

tHERE WERE SomE ups and downs

Many young soldiers from British Columbia and Vancouver were lost during World War I. After the war, the economy improved with the help of the recently opened Panama Canal, which allowed Vancouver and its port to prosper. Then the Great Depression hit and tough times struck. In 1939, World War II began. The Japanese attack on Pearl Harbor during the war had unfortunate consequences on Japanese Canadians, who were forced into internment camps far from the city. Restrictions were only lifted in 1949, when many returned to the coast.

vaNCouvER Got 'vaNCouvERizEd'

During the 1950s, Vancouver grew quickly. Many neighbourhoods outside downtown were established, and many residential areas near the centre were rezoned. Old houses were torn down in favour of apartments and parking lots. The streetcar and train lines were removed and replaced by roadways for a growing number of cars. Plans, including a huge freeway, were made that would completely change the city and its waterfront. Luckily, things moved slowly — nothing happened with this plan and, in the 1970s, times, the government, and plans, had all changed. The waterfront was saved from the freeway. Instead, it attracted thousands of pedestrians, and the city evolved in the unique 'Vancouverism' way.

Happy 100th birthday, Vancouver!

In 1986, Vancouver celebrated its 100th birthday with a large international exhibition. Expo 86 was a huge party that also started Vancouver's transformation into the city it is today. The fair's lasting legacies include the iconic Canada Place and Science World's giant 'golf ball', as well as the SkyTrain and BC Place.

Vancouver today

Construction hasn't stopped since Expo 86. Public transit continues to expand and buildings are continually being erected, creating one of the most impressive skylines in Canada. Vancouver is, and feels like, a young city with an informal, hip, and relaxed attitude. From the start, it has been a multicultural city, and continues to be today, with a particularly high number of Asian Vancouverites. The influence from the area's first inhabitants, the First Nations peoples, is also unmistakable. Vancouver has something for everyone and has developed into a world-class city. The 2010 Winter Olympic and Paralympic Games in Vancouver and Whistler are a testament to its success, and promise to be a blast!

Get Ready for your trip!

Tourism Vancouver's website (www.tourismvancouver.com) has all the information you'll need, including downloadable city and area maps. If you have any tips or questions for Junior Jetsetters, email us at: **FEEDBACK@JUNIORJETSETTERS.CA**.

olGa tHE oRca

baRt
tHE bald EaglE

Kai
tHE couga[b]

KEiRa

SEKANI
tHE SpiRit bEaR

KaSka
tHE caRibou

MiKE
tHE MuSKRat

joRdi

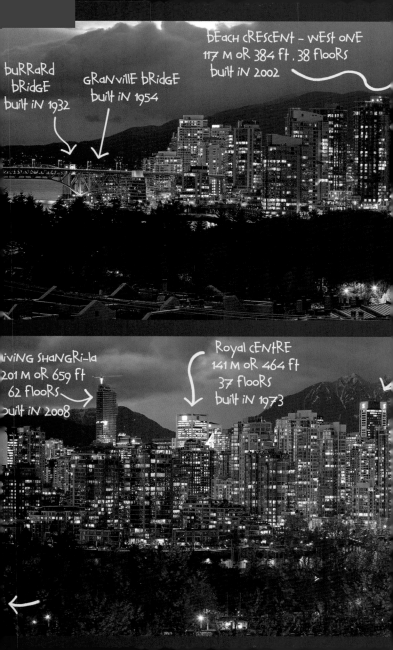

caN you staNd thE suspENsE?

Over a hundred years ago, a Park Commissioner for Vancouver bought land in Capilano to protect it from being logged. There was just one problem, though: the huge canyon down the middle. In 1889, he built a suspension bridge that attracted visitors from all over the world. The bridge has been replaced several times since then. These days, instead of being made of hemp rope, it uses 5 cm (2") steel cables. Plus, the planks of the bridge are replaced about every two years, so you can breathe easy knowing you're safe.

The Northwest Coast First Nations people have always had a strong connection to the land in and around Vancouver, and it's no different here. Kia'palano (the park's First Nations Cultural Centre) offers visitors the chance to meet some First Nations people and to learn about their culture and customs through traditional carvings, stories, and dance. Also, be sure not to miss the totem poles in the park. They're not just amazing works of art, but also serve an important purpose. First Nations people use totem poles to pass on legends from one generation to another.

After you've mustered up enough courage to walk across the bridge, be like a squirrel and take to the treetops. In the Treetops Adventure, you'll cross a network of suspension bridges hanging as high up as 30 metres in this West Coast rainforest. That is, if you're not afraid of heights…

You can also check out the gardens, nature trails, the Story Centre, The Living Forest, or the Cliffhanger Walk. And for an amazing photo, head over to Canyon Lookout. Or you could just dive in – so to speak – and join The Capilano Story Tour or Eco Tour for some in-depth knowledge.

cool, yEah?

The bridge is 137 metres (450 feet) long and hangs 70 metres (230 feet) above the canyon.

It's so strong that it can support two fully-loaded Boeing 747 aircraft.

a MaRKEt placE juSt foR Kids!

Granville Island is a small island in False Creek. The fact that the city of Vancouver's original name was Granville might lead you to believe that Vancouver started here, but that isn't the case. The truth is, the island didn't even exist back in 1886 when the city was incorporated!

When Granville Island was first established it was an industrial site with several factories that employed over a thousand workers. After World War II, demand for heavy industrial products declined and the area was gradually polluted by factories dumping toxic waste into the waters. Luckily, in the 1970s, the island was reclaimed by the city. These days, it's one of the hottest spots in town.

Here you'll find streets lined with the studios and workshops of artists and artisans. You're welcome to stop by to watch them create hand-made, one-of-a-kind pieces. The public market is also a huge draw with more than a hundred vendors selling pretty much everything… from fresh fish, to flowers, to crafts and candles. But Granville Island's got yet another market you won't want to miss – the Kids Market. Every food, shop and activity here is especially for kids and their families. The experience starts as soon as you walk through the kid-sized door! There's also a water park and playground for you to enjoy.

cool, yEah?

From Vancouver, don't take the bus or a car to get here! Grab a ferry or water taxi so you'll get the whole island experience.

Curious about the performers on the island? They're called the Granville Island Buskers. These local, national, and international performers really add to Granville Island's unique atmosphere. There are jugglers, dancers, magicians, and musicians from all over. Grab a seat and enjoy.

21

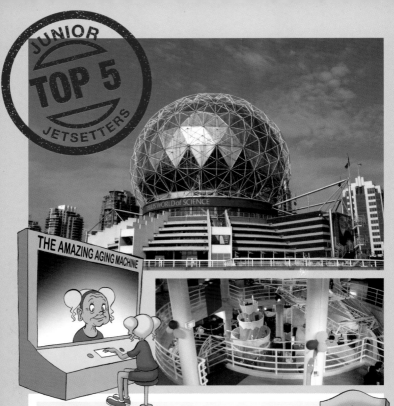

THE AMAZING AGING MACHINE

cool, yEaH?

Are you wondering what the difference is between OMNIMAX and IMAX: OMNIMAX theatres have dome screens, while IMAX theatres use rectangular screens. Both are pretty massive.

Just one cool thing you'll learn at Science World: Your eye muscles are the busiest muscles in your body and move over 100,000 times a day. And you don't even need gym class for that exercise!

22

a 40-METRE-HiGH Golf ball full of cool stuff

If you've seen Vancouver's skyline, you've probably noticed Science World. After all, it's pretty hard to miss a 40-metre (155-foot) high silver 'golf ball'! Of course, it isn't really a golf ball (sorry to disappoint you!). It's actually a geodesic dome, originally built as Expo 86's Expo Centre and later taken over by Science World.

Now you're probably wondering what's inside that huge dome. The top section is an OMNIMAX theatre, and it's really 'OmniHuge'. The dome is five storeys high, and the screen inside curves along with it. Make sure you catch a movie while you're there. The entire screen surrounds you, making you feel like you're right in the middle of the action! The rest of Science World is set up around a Centre Stage. Throughout the day, live science performances take place here, and kids are encouraged to participate. You'll learn about movement, electricity, cold, and toys. There's usually a surprise show, too!

As you wander through the building, you'll be amazed by how huge the place is, and how full of hands-on experiments it is. They aren't all about weird and crazy things, though. You'll see plenty of experiments that will relate to your everyday life. For example, one of the galleries is dedicated to 'Our World' and shows kids how they can make smart, environmental choices every day, now and in the future. And if you want to really get into science, the Eureka gallery is the place for you. Experiment with water, air, light, sound, motion, and machines. If you've ever asked the question: "What would happen if…?" then this is the place to get your answer.

cool, yEah?

Eastern grey squirrels are not native to British Columbia. They were introduced into Stanley Park in 1914 and are now found all over — but most of them are actually black!

a NatuRE lovER's paRadisE

Nature and parks have always been a priority in Vancouver. After Vancouver was incorporated in 1886 (that is, when the city became the city), one of the first decisions made by the City Council was to lease a 404-hectare (1,000 acre) peninsula from the Canadian Government and turn it into a park — Stanley Park, to be exact.

The land the park sits on today was originally home to the *Tsleil-Waututh* ('People of the Inlet' or Burrard), *Xʷməθkʷiʔəm* (Musqueam), and *Sḵwx̱wú7mesh* (Squamish) First Nations peoples, who had many villages in the area. Because food and other materials were plentiful, it was an ideal place for them. The large cedar trees were perfect for making canoes and longhouses. And the coast was perfect for fishing.

Sometime after the British arrived, they decided that the peninsula was a strategic military location and the area was designated as a military reserve. It was later logged for several years. Luckily, because of its military designation, the land was left undeveloped, and has remained so under Vancouver Parks & Recreation.

Today the park is a nature lovers' paradise with beaches, lakes, lagoons, a rainforest full of monument trees (the oldest trees in the park), and plenty of trails, including the famous Seawall (SEE PaGE 66). The park is home to many animals, like raccoons, coyotes, rabbits, skunks, and grey squirrels. You'll also find many types of birds living here, such as bald eagles, swans, geese, ducks, and blue herons, as well as many other species during migrating season.

JUNIO
TOP
JETSE

WE DARE you: say you'RE boRED

Stanley Park is packed with a ridiculous number of activities — almost too many for one kid to handle! If you're the sporty type, you can hit the tennis courts, sink a hole-in-one on the pitch and putt golf course, take a swim in the pool, rollerblade, bike, walk, or just spend some time running around in one of the playgrounds.

If you're an arty kind of kid, you won't want to miss the Painters' Circle. It's like an outdoor art gallery where local landscape artists can sit down to paint or display the works they've already created. Feeling dramatic? During the summer, you can attend an outdoor evening performance of Theatre Under the Stars.

If animals are your thing, stop by the Salmon Stream for an explanation of the spawning process and the annual salmon run. (SEE PaGE 38 foR MoRE about tHE SalMoN RuN.) Walk through the children's farmyard and visit over 200 barnyard animals and birds before hitching a ride on the miniature railway.

cool, yEaH?

One of the most popular attractions in the park is the totem pole display. There are eight impressive totem poles, each with a story to tell.

The park is also home to monuments and sculptures: Air India Monument, Girl in a Wet Suit, Japanese Monument, Shakespeare Garden, SS Beaver Cairn, SS Empress of Japan, as well as tons of sculptures of important people, like Queen Victoria and her Governor General of Canada, and Lord Stanley (recognize the name?).

Like we said, there's a lot to see and do. Since your feet will probably get tired from all that walking, hop on the old-fashioned horse-drawn tram. While the horses trot through the park, your guide will explain what you're seeing and tell you cool stories along the way.

And, last but not least, if you want a spectacular view of the North Shore Mountains, head over to the tip of Stanley Park. Here, you'll find Prospect Point — the farthest point in the park from downtown. Relax a little and enjoy the scenery while you eat a hand-packed ice cream cone. After all, you need a break. You've had a seriously busy day!

Kla-how-Eya: WElcomE!

Long before Europeans 'discovered' and settled the West Coast, First Nations peoples lived on this land. The waters were full of fish to eat and made for a great way to get from one place to another (by boat); the forests provided materials for building shelters and plants that were used for food and medicine; animals could be hunted for meat; and the mild climate made it an ideal place to live year-round. It was a comfortable life, and besides pursuing cultural, religious, and social activities, the First Nations peoples also made some incredible art.

Not only did this art look really cool, it also contained meaningful symbols and told important stories that would be passed from one generation to the next. Even after the Europeans arrived, the Indigenous peoples remained in the area. The influence and impact they had (and continue to have) on Vancouver is undeniable. You can't go very far without seeing a totem pole, a painting, or some other Aboriginal item.

The Vancouver area was home to three First Nations peoples: *Sḵwx̱wú7mesh* (Squamish), *Tsleil-Waututh* ('People of the Inlet' or Burrard), and *X̱ʷməθkʷiʔəm* (Musqueam). They established settlements and villages, many of which still exist today. There are about 200,000 First Nations people in British Columbia, making up 198 communities or bands.

If you want to experience First Nations culture while in Vancouver, you'll have tons of choices. Galleries, museums, and cultural centres are located throughout the city. The Bill Reid Gallery (SEE PaGE 32) and the Museum of Anthropology (SEE PaGE 54) are great places to learn more about First Nations peoples and several art galleries can be found in Gastown (SEE PaGE 48).

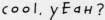

cool, yEaH?

These groups of people were once called Indians – a term which came about after Christopher Columbus, landing in the Americas for the first time, actually believed he'd landed in India! Today, the name First Nations is much preferred.

JUNIOR
TOP 5
JETSETTERS

a MuSEuM wHERE you'RE SuRE to bREaK a SwEat

The BC Sports Hall of Fame, in BC Place (the huge dome-shaped stadium that is home to the BC Lions football team) honours British Columbia's athletes and teams. Here, you'll have a chance to learn about thrilling sports stories, such as Terry Fox's.

Terry Fox grew up in Vancouver and Port Coquitlam in British Columbia. He loved sports. But at the age of 18, he was in a car crash and hurt his knee. Shortly after the accident, cancer was found in that knee. The only way to treat it at that time was to remove his leg. But Terry Fox would not let that beat him. To raise money for cancer research, he decided to run from coast to coast. He called this run the Marathon of Hope. In April, 1980, he started in St. John's, Newfoundland, where he dipped his leg into the Atlantic Ocean, and his destination was the Pacific Ocean in Victoria, B.C. But unfortunately, by the time he reached Ontario, doctors discovered that the cancer had spread to his lungs and he was forced to stop. Even though he didn't complete the cross-country journey, over $24 million was raised — $1 for every Canadian. He quickly became a national icon. And the Terry Fox Run (an annual charity event) is now held in over 50 countries around the world.

If you're at all into sports, you'll love wandering through the galleries learning other cool stories of bravery and sportsmanship like this one, but you'll also do way more than just stand around looking at stuff. This is a museum where you can actually break a sweat! Test your own athletic abilities on the climbing wall, the virtual sports simulators, the radar-enhanced running track, or even the foosball table!

cool, yEah?

The Olympic Inspirations exhibit highlights how well British Columbia has done in the Olympics over the years.

BC Place is the site of the Opening and Closing Ceremonies of the 2010 Olympic Winter Games and the Opening Ceremony of the Paralympic Games.

31

all Hail tHE totEm maN!

Bill Reid is one of the most well-known artists of Haida descent. The Haida are a First Nations people who originally made their home on the Queen Charlotte Islands (a cluster of about 150 islands) north of Vancouver.

Because they came from islands, the Haida have always had a strong relationship with water. They were known as great seamen and developed a special canoe for ocean travel. These canoes were carved from single giant red cedars and — measuring as much as 18 metres (60 feet) — could hold 60 paddlers, making them ideal for long-distance travel, offshore fishing, and sea mammal hunting. The Haida have also been credited with being the first to use the totem pole as a cultural symbol.

In the 1950s, a young man and soon-to-be artist became very interested in these sculptures and started to salvage totem poles that had been abandoned. This artist was Bill Reid, who went on to become one of the most renowned Northwest Coast artists. His art, some of which he created in his studio on Granville Island (SEE PaGE 2o), can be seen all over the city, including at the airport and outside the Vancouver Aquarium (SEE PaGE 72).

But you can also see tons of it (as well as the work of other Northwest Coast Aboriginal artists) at the Bill Reid Gallery. You can even a see a new totem pole which was carved in 2008 to celebrate Reid's influence on other Indigenous artists.

32

cool, yEah?

The Haida prospered on the Queen Charlotte Islands (also called Haida Gwaii) until they came into contact with Europeans in the late 1700s. Over the next two hundred years, diseases (especially smallpox) brought by the Europeans wiped out about 95 per cent of the Haida population.

One of Bill Reid's most famous sculptures is The Spirit of Haida Gwaii, which depicts a canoe filled with humans and animals. The back of the Canadian $20 bill includes an image of this sculpture.

HOW HORTICULTURAL ARE YOU?

Like a lot of Vancouver, the area where Queen Elizabeth Park is today was once owned by the Canadian Pacific Railway. Back in the early 1900s, this spot was the highest point of land in the city and was a basalt (a type of rock) quarry. The rock excavated was used to build roads until the quarry closed in 1911. The land was then sold to the city but it wasn't until shortly after King George VI of England, and his wife Queen Elizabeth, visited Vancouver in 1939 that the place was renamed Queen Elizabeth Park.

The garden you see today is the result of the work of one man with a vision. William Livingstone, a deputy superintendent, designed the park. Instead of filling in the quarries, he used them to display plants and water features. The main Quarry Garden is one of the highlights of the park; another is the Arboretum on the slopes surrounding the quarries.

Painters' Corner is an outdoor gallery with art by landscape artists who work on-site. And the Celebration Pavilion and dancing water fountains are perfect places to take a picture or two. In fact, you might spot a few couples posing for wedding photos there! If looking at pretty flowers isn't your thing, there's also a lawn bowling club, disc (Frisbee) golf, a pitch and putt golf course and putting green, and a whole bunch of tennis courts. After a busy day, stop by the restaurant for a quick bite to eat.

If your green thumb is still itching for more, stop by the Bloedel Floral Conservatory (also in the park). Inside this domed structure, you'll find a colourful tropical garden, complete with Koi fish, parrots, and over 100 free-flying tropical birds. Pick up a self-guided tour map and make your way through the garden. If you have time, walk through more than once. There's always something new to see!

cool, yEaH?

When designing the park, William Livingstone did not work from drawings — the entire plan was simply in his mind.

The Arboretum will one day display one tree of every species native to Canada (well, those that can live in Vancouver's climate).

cool, yEaH?

Vancouver is only the second of two Canadian cities to hold the world exposition – the other was Montréal for Expo 67.

Port Metro Vancouver is the busiest port in Canada with over 3,000 ships arriving every year and over 100 million tonnes of cargo moving through it.

bizaRRE boat buildiNG, aHoy!

As Vancouver's 100th birthday approached, the city decided to celebrate with a big party and exposition — but as the plans developed, it became clear that the celebration was going to be a really big deal — a world exposition, in fact. In 1983, construction of buildings for Expo 86 began.

The most famous, and most photographed, of these buildings is Canada Place. Used as the Canadian Pavilion during the Expo, it is now a cruise ship terminal, an IMAX movie theatre, a convention centre, a restaurant, and a hotel, as well as the Interpretive Centre for Port Metro Vancouver (the city's port). It doesn't really look like a building though, so it will be easy for you to spot. It sticks out into Burrard Inlet and looks like a huge ship with its sails up. The whole thing is quite a sight, especially when a cruise ship is docked next to it.

Events are held here year-round, although the Canada Day and Christmas celebrations are the highlights of the year, with Canada Day being the largest event on the West Coast. Try taking a 'promenade' along Canada Place. You'll learn about Vancouver's unique history, its beautiful location, its native legends and other stories, its multi-deck luxury cruise ships and ginormous cargo ships, and how all of these things make Vancouver the city that it is today. And if you're really into ships, don't miss Port Metro Vancouver's Interpretive Centre. Not only will you learn all about the types of ships that sail by Vancouver, you can actually watch them pass by on their way in and out of port.

CANADA PLACE

wAtCH a fiSH RuN uP a laddER

The fishing industry (SEE PaGE 134) has always played a big part in the growth and history of British Columbia, but salmon — because there are so many on the West Coast — have played a huge part.

Here are a few fishy facts for you: salmon are born in fresh water and then make their way out into the salty water of the ocean. They return to fresh water, swimming up the river against the flow, to reproduce – this is known as the salmon run. A large and historic salmon run used to occur in the Capilano River every year. This river, which flows through the Coast Mountains, also provides a lot of the drinking water for people in Greater Vancouver. To help get this water to the people, a dam was built in the 1950s (SEE PaGE 42). But while the dam was great for the people, it was bad news for the salmon, who could no longer make their way upstream. At first, the salmon swimming upstream were collected, transported in tanks, and then released above the dam, where they could continue their journey. This solved one problem, but created another – many of the young salmon didn't survive the trip back downstream over the dam.

The salmon population quickly decreased. To help the salmon out, a hatchery (a place where fish eggs are hatched) was built about 500 metres from the dam. Capilano's hatchery conducts scientific research and also educates the public about salmon and the importance of the hatchery. There's also a fish ladder, which is a sort of canal that allows the salmon to swim upstream without facing the dangers of the dam. Spawning season varies by salmon type, but the best time to visit is in the summer and autumn, when the fish are most active. During peak times, the ladder is completely full of 'running' fish swimming upstream.

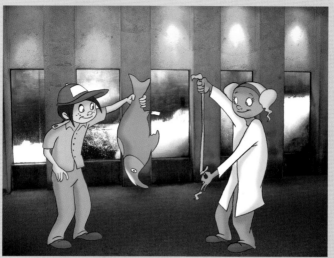

cool, yEaH?

When they're ready to spawn, salmon return to the exact spot where they were born. They never forget it. After spawning, most salmon die.

The hatchery releases over 1 million smolts (young fish) every year. About 15,000 return to spawn.

cool, yEaH?

Dim sum is a breakfast or lunch meal that consists of various steamed dishes, pastries, barbecued meat, buns, and dumplings. Don't expect a menu when you eat dim sum – the food comes in bamboo steamers that you order off carts that are pushed around the restaurant.

dim sum, cool shops, and the tiniest building you'll see

Vancouver is home to the largest Chinatown in Canada. This area is also one of the city's earliest communities. The first Chinese came to British Columbia from California during the gold rush way back in 1858, in search of a better life. Often, their work was seasonal and they came to Vancouver between jobs. Many worked in construction (building roads and railroads), some worked in the lumber industry, while many others were involved in the fishing and canning industry. Many men would bring their wives and children over once they had saved enough money. But, in 1903 the head tax was raised to $500 and most Chinese men were no longer able to afford to bring their families. Instead, they sent money back home and often went to visit.

Given its long history, it's not surprising that Chinatown has several historic landmarks. One of the easiest to spot is the Millennium Gate—the gateway into Chinatown. And the Sam Kee Company is definitely one building you'll want to see. But be careful, it's so narrow that you just might miss it if you blink! A merchant, Chang Toy, originally owned a nine-metre lot here. Unfortunately, in 1912, the city decided to widen Pender Street and took over most of the property. Furious at the city, Chang Toy built a 1.8 metre (6 foot) office building on the land!

Other cool sites include the Chinese Cultural Centre, the Dr. Sun Yat-Sen Park and Classical Chinese Garden (SEE PAGE 46), Historical Alley, and the Monument of Canadian Chinese. If you're craving dim sum, look no further. New Town Bakery & Restaurant is a best bet and is famous for its steamed buns.

taKE tHE daM pictuRE!

The Capilano River is an important river in North Vancouver. It flows through the Coast Mountains (a huge mountain range that stretches from the Yukon, through Alaska, and down the entire coast of British Columbia), and empties into Burrard Inlet, opposite Stanley Park (SEE PaGE 24). The river provides about 40 per cent of the drinking water for the Greater Vancouver area.

In order to supply water to the growing Vancouver area, the river was partially dammed in 1889. In 1954, the Cleveland Dam was built, creating a huge reservoir, now called Capilano Lake. The area surrounding the lake is closed to the public to protect the quality of the water, but the view from the dam is amazing, offering a close-up of the Lions (a pair of pointed mountain peaks). It's definitely worth a picture!

Downstream you'll find the Capilano River Regional Park. The park contains the Capilano Salmon Hatchery (SEE PaGE 38) as well as 8 kilometres (5 miles) of hiking and biking trails running along the river through the coastal rainforest. The river flows through a granite canyon, and attracts fishermen, kayakers, and canoers. But, be warned, the water can move fast here. It's definitely not for beginners.

cool, yEaH?

> **The park and the dam are often used for movies and television shows. The dam was a key setting in one episode of Smallville.**
>
> **The river can get quite fast and is rated as a class III river (on a scale of I to V).**

Important Note: The canyon can be a very dangerous place for people of all ages because of the steep and slippery banks that lie within. Some areas of the canyon are marked with signs and fenced off. Remember that it's possible for the water level to become dangerously high within a short period of time. Be aware. It is not possible to safeguard the entire park. Do not leave your parents' side during your visit and do not take risks.

43

WHERE YOUR PARENTS WILL LET YOU RIDE A MOTORCYCLE...SORT OF

Did you know that the motorcycle was invented by accident? Two German inventors were working on a gas-powered engine. To see if it worked, they needed something to attach the engine onto, so they decided to use a bicycle. This motorized bike eventually became the first motorcycle.

Harley-Davidson was one of the earliest motorcycle makers in North America. Unlike other motorcycles that are used for sports or racing, Harleys (that's what most people call them) are designed for cruising on the highway. They are so awesome and their engines have such a unique sound that people often stare at them even when they're going at 20 km/h. What's more, they're often customized by and for their owners. Owners of Harleys are very loyal and have their own clubs and events. For them, riding a motorcycle is more than a way to get around — it's a way of life.

In 1917, the Deeley family, who owned a motorcycle business in Vancouver, became a Harley-Davidson dealership. The grandson of the founder took his interest in motorcycles even further than the rest of the family. He not only sold them but raced them as well. He also started a collection which wasn't limited to Harleys. It's made up of over 250 vintage (antique) motorcycles of 59 different makes, some dating back over a hundred years.

If you're not sure what all the fuss is about, maybe it's because you've never ridden on a motorcycle before. No problem — check out the museum's Orbital Map with interactive touch screens and experience a virtual ride across British Columbia. Then you'll get it.

cool, yEaH?

The inventors of the motorcycle never actually commercially produced motorcycles. They went on to produce some of the first cars. Their company went on to become Daimler-Benz, the maker of Mercedes-Benz.

At one time, Harleys were nicknamed 'Hogs' after a team of farm boys in the 1920s who won a lot of races. Their mascot was a hog and they would put a real pig on their Harleys during their victory laps. Today it's become a term referring to all large motorcycles.

cool, yEah?

The garden was built using authentic techniques, dating back to Ming dynasty gardens, by craftsmen from Suzhou, China, and Canada. The construction of the halls and walkways did not involve the use of any nails, screws, or glue – only precise joinery!

a little bit of yin and a little bit of yang

For years, Vancouver has attracted many visitors from China. One of these visitors was a doctor nam Sun Yat-Sen, who is known as the 'Father of Mode China' because of his role in bringing democracy t the country in the early 20th century. He travelled t world to help promote the pro-democracy moveme raising support and money. His travels brought him Vancouver three times. In 1911, he led the revoluti that eventually overthrew the Qing dynasty and, in 1912, he became the first president of the Republi China.

In honour of Dr. Sun Yat-Sen, a park and classical Chinese garden were created in time for Expo 86. garden is made up of four main elements that com together in perfect balance. This reflects the princi of *yin* and *yang*, opposites that work together to create balance and harmony in Chinese landscape architecture, and Chinese culture in general. These elements are: rock, water, plants, and architecture.

The limestone rocks, which were brought from Chi and appear to change colour, are believed to bring lucky spirits into the garden. The jade-green water a central part of the garden and is the soft balance (*yin*) to the rocks' hard edges (*yang*). The plants in the garden are a mix of native Chinese and local plants, and are believed to have mystical powers. The architecture has been designed to blend into the natural environment. Several small pavilions throughout the garden let visitors spend time alone and the larger pavilions are perfect places to gathe and enjoy the setting.

a man named John Deighton arrived on the south
Burrard Inlet. He opened a saloon in the area
the time, there was nothing but a lumber mill. His
to make money serving alcohol to the workers.
ton was well-known for the tall tales he told. In
earned him the nickname 'Gassy Jack', since his
ries seemed like a bunch of hot air to most people!
of Gassy Jack and his saloon, the area soon
known as Gastown. It wasn't the nicest name,
o not long after the town renamed it Granville. Of
at didn't stop people from calling it by its original
h funnier) name.

Gastown…er, Granville, was incorporated as the
ncouver. By this time, the city had grown and had
buildings. Unfortunately, not long after, the Great
r Fire broke out and all but two buildings burned
he ground. Then the depression hit and the area
ically forgotten until the 1960s. Plans were even
ear the place down but, luckily, a group of citizens
er to save Gastown and, in 1971, it was declared
area.

yEaH?

*The most famous landmark in Gastown is the
eam clock, which was built to cover a steam grate.
It harnesses the power of the steam. Don't be
fooled - it's not as old as you would think.*

*Jack made a deal with the mill workers – he
sell them whiskey if they built him his saloon.
oon was up and ready in just one day!!!*

During its heyday, Gastown was full of bars, but now things have changed. The area is a popular spot for tourists and Vancouverites alike, with fashion, furniture, art shops, restaurants, and all sorts of sidewalk stands selling stuff to tourists. There are also plenty of art galleries and several events throughout the year, including a bike race, motorbike and classic car shows, and a jazz festival.

Fly liKE a biRd, oR visit a bEaR

At first glance, Grouse Mountain looks like a regular ski hill close to downtown Vancouver. And it is well-known for its skiing. But Grouse Mountain offers tons more to do, in winter and in summer. Your visit begins with a ride up the mountain on the Skyride gondola. On your way up, you'll see the Cascade and Olympic mountains, Vancouver Island, the city of Vancouver, and the Pacific Ocean. You'll arrive at the Peak Chalet, 1,128 metres (3,700 feet) above Vancouver.

Now imagine flying high above the rainforest, at 80 km/h, with your feet dangling. If that doesn't make you queasy, you might be interested in ziplining, one of the most breathtaking activities at Grouse Mountain. Or what about mountain paragliding? Learn basic flight techniques and meteorology (study of weather) and then enjoy a 15-20 minute flight with an expert instructor. You'll feel like a bird, hundreds of feet above the trees, using the same thermal currents they do!

Nearby, you can stop by the Grizzly Bear Habitat and visit Grinder and Coola, two famous grizzlies that were rescued in 2001 when they were young cubs. In the summer, check out the Lumberjack Show or Birds in Motion, featuring some of the fastest birds in the world. Join one of the walking tours, or explore the mountain on your own (well, with your parents!).

The activities in the winter are just as fun. Of course there's skiing, but you can also try showshoeing, ice skating, sno-limo rides, winter ziplining, and a popular holiday tradition called the Peak of Christmas, featuring Santa's workshop, sleigh rides, reindeer, and Christmas movies.

Before going back down the mountain, hop on the Peak Chair Lift and head up to the top. You'll reach 1,250 metres (4,100 feet)! Whichever activities you choose, get ready for a high altitude experience.

GRouSE GRiNd

In the summer, forget the Skyride. If you're in good shape and are ready for a challenge, try the Grouse Grind. 'Mother Nature's Stairmaster', as it is often called, is a trail that heads up the mountain with 2,830 steps over 2.9 kilometres (1.8 miles).

The Grind will probably take you a couple of hours, so plan ahead with proper hiking gear, water, snacks, and clothes for the changing weather. Visit www.grousemountain.com/Summer/ mountain-report for conditions and updates.

ERS

GEt aliENatEd!!!

Have you ever wondered if life exists on other planets? Or what aliens might look like? How about what you might look like if you were an alien? The H.R. MacMillan Space Centre will actually show you! The centre has a cool computer that takes into account several factors that you select (such as the planet size and water content) and combines them with your photo. How's that for an alien experience?

On a visit to the space centre, you'll also get a chance to see the stars. When you visit the planetarium, Harold the projector will show you the Vancouver sky like you've never seen it before! From there, head over to GroundStation Canada for your chance to find out about Canada's role in space and to learn about what is actually going on up there. You'll discover how astronauts eat, sleep, and even go to the bathroom in space.

And if you've ever dreamed of flying a space shuttle, the Cosmic Courtyard is for you. There are tons of activities and video games where you can, for instance, test your piloting skills by docking a space shuttle yourself! And if you're around on a clear Saturday night, head over to the Gordon MacMillan Southam Observatory for a chance to look through a real telescope. Finally, take a trip in the Virtual Voyages Motion Simulator. After you receive your mission, you'll climb aboard a small spacecraft. Trust us, you don't want to miss this simulation (just remember to buckle up!).

cool, yEah?

Many people think that the building looks like a spaceship. But, actually, it was designed to resemble the hats of the Haida (SEE PaGE 32).

The crab statue outside the Space Centre also comes from the Haida. Legend says that the crab is the protector of the harbour.

tHE RavEN aNd tHE FiRSt MEN

The Raven and the First Men *tells the story of human creation. One day, the Raven (the most powerful mythical creature in Haida culture) came across an interesting clamshell on a beach. Coming out of the shell were several small human beings. Although they were hesitant at first, the Raven was able to persuade the humans to leave the shell and join him in his world. The legend says those humans were the first Haida.*

tOWERiNG tOtEMS aNd So MUCH MoRE

Have you ever heard of a museum in a basement? Well, that's exactly how this one started over 50 years ago. But today the collection is housed above ground in a cool-looking glass-panelled building, inspired by traditional Northwest Coast post-and-beam style architecture. It's fitting since this museum specializes in the cultures of Indigenous peoples around the world. Most of the objects here come from the Northwest Coast First Nations peoples. And the most impressive items in the museum are definitely the massive totem poles in the Great Hall, which look especially awesome against the mountains in the background.

A big part of the museum's collection is made up of stuff that once belonged to ancient Indigenous peoples, however, works of art by Northwest Coast First Nations artists are also featured, and so are items from East and South Asia, the South Pacific, the Americas, Africa, and Europe. One gallery is dedicated to European ceramics, while others are used for temporary exhibitions. One of the highlights of the museum is the Rotunda. There, you can see one of the most important First Nations sculptures, *The Raven and the First Men*, by Bill Reid (SEE PaGE 32). A drawing of the sculpture now appears on the Canadian $20 bill. (If you're lucky enough that your allowance includes one of those, it might look familiar to you.)

Outside the museum, you can explore a replica of a 19th century Haida village. The 'village' contains a large family dwelling and a small mortuary house that would have been used traditionally for keeping dead bodies. In front of the houses are several totem poles, some of which were carved by Bill Reid.

STEP iNto a SpacEShip aNd CHEcK out vaNcouvER's HiStoRy

From the minute you set foot inside the Museum of Vancouver, you'll think you've travelled back in time. But, as you approach the building, you might feel more like you've been beamed into the future. "What is that giant white spaceship doing in the park?" you will probably ask yourself. Strange as it may seem, that's the museum. (It shares space with the H.R. MacMillan Space Centre (SEE paGE 52), which *might* explains the odd shape).

For such a young city, Vancouver's history is pretty colourful. At the Museum of Vancouver you'll journey through time, starting at the turn of the 20th century. (Of course, there were people in the Vancouver area before that — SEE paGE 28.)

You'll learn about the Nikkei, who were Canadians of Japanese heritage. Many were involved in the fishing industry and made up a large portion of the population of Steveston (SEE paGE 134), but others lived in Vancouver. In fact, a thriving Japanese community lived on Powell Street. Back then, women weren't allowed to run mainstream businesses. Nikkei were considered second-class citizens — even those who had lived in Canada for generations. In Japan, however, young women were taught sewing as a basic skill before marriage, which proved useful in Canada. These women could, and did, set up tailoring and dressmaking shops. Powell Street was full of them! Unfortunately, like all Japanese in the area, after the attack on Pearl Harbor in World War II, Japanese-Canadians were sent to internment camps.

But Vancouver's past isn't all that dark. The museum has a huge collection of cool, fun, interesting, and downright weird items from different periods. For instance, have you ever seen a jukebox? Check out the 50s gallery for your chance to pick a tune.

cool, yEah?

During the 1950s, Vancouver had a lot of neon signs. It may be hard to believe, but at one time, it had more than Las Vegas!

You might notice an old black-and-white movie playing above you. It's the oldest video footage of Vancouver, filmed back in 1907. You'll recognize some of the buildings, which are still standing today.

WHERE athletes go for gold!

Plans for Vancouver/Whistler to host the Olympic Winter Games were in the works for decades. The area was a finalist to host the 1976 Games, which were eventually held in Innsbruck, Austria. Then another chance came in 1998, for the 2010 Games. This time, Vancouver beat out another Austrian city (Salzburg) and was selected by the International Olympic Committee as the host.

The Olympic Winter Games include seven sports (and 86 medal events): biathlon, bobsleigh and skeleton, curling, ice hockey, luge, skating (figure and speed), and skiing (alpine, cross-country, freestyle, Nordic combined, ski-jump, and

snowboard). The Paralympic Winter Games include five sports (and 46 medal events): alpine skiing, biathlon, cross-country skiing, ice sledge hockey, and wheelchair curling.

The venues for the Olympic and Paralympic Games are split between Vancouver (and surrounding cities Richmond, Surrey, and West Vancouver) and Whistler, and include BC Place Stadium, Cypress Mountain (SEE PAGE 118), and, of course, Whistler Mountain (SEE PAGE 144). The Vancouver Village is located on False Creek near Science World (SEE PAGE 22) and the Whistler Village is in the Cheakamus Valley in the Coast Mountains, 624 metres above sea level.

cool, yEah?

Vancouver was chosen to host the Olympic and Paralympic Winter Games, even though it rarely snows in the city.

Canada has hosted the Olympic Games twice before (the Summer Games in Montréal, Québec in 1976 and the Winter Games in Calgary, Alberta in 1988) and the Paralympic Games once (the Summer Games in Toronto, Ontario in 1976).

REady, SEt, play!

Playland is Vancouver's amusement park. It's been around for almost 100 years, but only became known as Playland in 1958 when it moved to the present site in Hastings Park. That year, the park introduced a roller coaster, which is Playland's signature attraction. It's over 50 years old and still the most popular ride. But don't be fooled. Just because it's old, doesn't mean it's slow! The ride reaches speeds of up to 75 km/h — fast enough to make your face look like a pancake.

Of course, the roller coaster isn't the only ride. What would an amusement park be without a Ferris wheel, a swinging pirate ship, bumper cars, or a log ride? And if you're after a real thrill, and heights don't scare you, there's always Drop Zone or the Hellevator (you know you want to try it!). There are also games, attractions, and all types of snacks.

If you're at Playland at the end of the summer, you're in for a treat. For the 17 days leading up to Labour Day, the Pacific National Exhibition holds its annual Fair. The original fair, which opened in 1910, was organized as a way to promote the city, its beauty, and its future. Although it started mostly as a way for the city to showcase industrial advancements, today it's a place for entertainment. Vancouverites and visitors love to browse through the shops and stalls and to take in the performances, live shows, and fireworks displays.

cool, yEaH?

During World War II, the Pacific National Exhibition (like its eastern counterpart, Toronto's Canadian National Exhibition) served as a military training facility.

If you're a video-game-a-holic, start flexing your thumbs now! At Command Headquarters in the Arcade, you'll find the latest games from around the world.

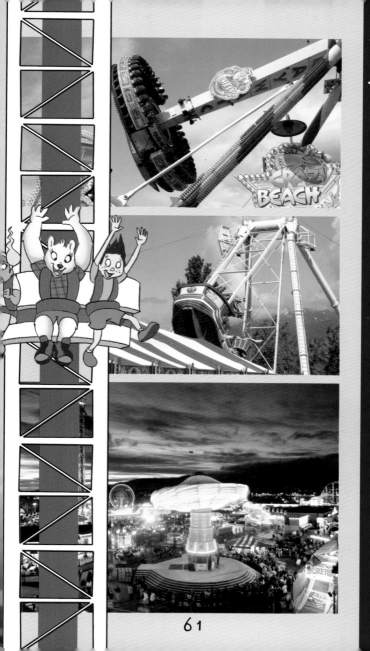

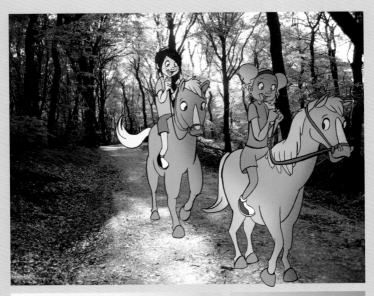

cool, yEah?

The parks also offer organized acivities including canoeing, hiking, pilates, and yoga!

aN awEsomE amouNt of outdooRsy activity

If you haven't already realized it, Vancouver is a pretty outdoorsy city. So it's not surprising that there are more than a few regional parks nearby. Actually, there are 21 in Metro Vancouver, to be exact! Just like the geography of the city itself, these parks are super-diverse. They include beaches, valleys, mountains, and forests and can range in size from as small as six hectares to a huge 3,700.

The closest ones are Capilano River Regional Park (SEE PaGE 42) to the north, and Pacific Spirit Regional Park, which surrounds the University of British Columbia campus to the south. If you've been to the UBC Botanical Garden or Nitobe Memorial Garden (SEE PaGE 70), or to the Museum of Anthropology (SEE PaGE 54), then you've probably stumbled upon Pacific Spirit already.

Each park has something different to offer, including picnic areas, camp sites, viewing towers, fish hatcheries, heritage buildings, canoeing and kayaking, fishing, swimming, beaches, tennis courts, and horseback riding. If you're looking for a particular activity, visit the Metro Vancouver website (see the reference section for the web address) where you can search for the best park for you and your family.

Remember, it's the wild, and there are some potential dangers out there, such as sudden climate changes and some ferocious animals! Take precautions, dress accordingly, carry enough water, and always, always, always leave your route and schedule with someone back in the city... just in case!

bE SEEN at tHE HiPPEst HaNGOuts aNd coolEst cafEs

Robson Street is one of the main streets of downtown Vancouver and is the most popular destination for shoppers. The street is lined with the hippest hangouts, coolest cafés, and chicest shops. Don't be surprised if you see some rich and famous visitors while strolling down Robson. It's also the place to see exotic cars and all sorts of motorcycles. It might also be the only place where you'll find two Starbucks coffee shops on opposite corners of the same intersection!

Robson Street stretches from BC Place all the way to Stanley Park (SEE paGE 24). Close to the middle of the street stands Robson Square. This square is a combination civic centre-public plaza. Within it are a UBC campus, offices, restaurants, public spaces, gardens, waterfalls, and, in the winter, an ice-skating rink. You'll also see some truly weird stairs! The Provincial Law Courts and the Vancouver Art Gallery (SEE paGE 74) stand at opposite ends of the square.

The square is a quiet get-away, right in the heart of the city. Thanks to the trees and waterfalls, you won't hear the noise of the city around the square. In fact, it's the perfect place to get out of downtown, without leaving downtown.

cool, yEaH?

At one time, a section of Robson Street was the centre of German culture and business in the city, earning it the nickname **Robsonstrasse** *(Robson Street, in German). The city even placed Robsonstrasse street signs!*

Original plans for the area were completely different and included building the tallest skyscraper in the city. Those plans changed when a new government came into power in the 1970s.

cool, yEah?

Construction of the Seawall employed thousands of people. During the 1920s, at a time of high unemployment, 2,300 men were kept busy building it.

66

COME SEE tHE SEa aNd tHEN walk tHE wall

To get into Burrard Inlet, large ships have to pass through the First Narrows (the narrow body of water between the tip of Stanley Park and the south shore of North Vancouver). From a very early time, people knew that the increasing ship traffic would affect the shores of Stanley Park. The passing ships would create waves that would slowly erode the northern shore of the park. To prevent this, the city and the Canadian Government decided to build a seawall around the park. Construction lasted a long time – more than 65 years!

Even though the original plan was to protect the shore, eventually the Park Board decided to put a proper surface on the wall and to create a path for walkers, joggers, and bicyclists.

And it turns out this was a fantastic idea! Today the path is one of the most popular features of Stanley Park. The seawall around the park is nearly 9 km (5.5 miles) long and is now only one piece of a pathway that connects Vancouver's entire inner waterfront. That's a 22-kilometre path that starts at Coal Harbour, then winds around Stanley Park, English Bay Beach and Sunset Beach, False Creek (including Granville Island), and Vanier Park, ending at Kitsilano Beach.

On a hot summer day, you'll join thousands of Vancouverites making use of this unique path. Just remember to pay attention to the signs and marks on the path — one side (or lane) is for walkers, while the other is for cyclists and rollerbladers. You can imagine how many accidents there must have been before they came up with this two lane system!

FEELING SPORTY?
THEN TAKE TO THE STANDS!

If you're into keeping active, Vancouver's got plenty to offer, both indoors and out. But if you love the thrill of a close game, the roar of a crowd, and the taste of a giant, concession stand hot dog slathered in ketchup, you're also in luck. Vancouver and the surrounding area are home to several sports teams. They include the BC Lions, the Vancouver Canucks, the Vancouver Whitecaps FC, and several lacrosse teams of the Western Lacrosse Association.

The **BC Lions** are a Canadian football team. People often refer to this sport as American football (as opposed to European football, which North Americans usually call soccer), even though Canadian football has many differences from its American cousin. The BC Lions play in BC Place Stadium, a huge stadium whose domed roof is supported by air.

COOL, YEAH?

While the goal of American football teams is to win the Superbowl, Canadian football teams play to win the Grey Cup. The BC Lions have won this championship five times, most recently in 2006.

Sporting venues cannot have corporate marks during the Olympics. So for the 2010 Winter Olympic Games, GM Place's name is Canada Hockey Place.

The **Vancouver Canucks** are the city's National Hockey League team. As in the rest of the country, Canadians' love of (ice) hockey is obvious in Vancouver. The team plays in General Motors Place (GM Place), across the street from BC Place Stadium.

If you want to watch soccer (or football as it's known outside North America) head over to Burnaby to catch the **Vancouver Whitecaps FC** (Football Club). The Whitecaps will join the Major League Soccer in 2011, at which time they'll play in BC Place Stadium.

For another truly Canadian experience, don't miss seeing a lacrosse match. Lacrosse can be either outdoor (called field lacrosse) or indoor (box lacrosse). British Columbia has several box lacrosse teams around Vancouver, all part of the **Western Lacrosse Association**. Lacrosse is based on a game originally played by the *Haudenosaunee* (Iroquois) in eastern Canada near the St. Lawrence. Teams include the Burnaby Lakers, Coquitlam Adanacs, Langley Thunder, Maple Ridge Burrards, New Westminster Salmonbellies.

stop to SMEll tHE flowERs tHEN take a walk up iN tHE tREEs

Plants are important for so many things — food, medicine, clothing, and fuel, just to name a few. They've been on the Earth for millions of years — even before dinosaurs. You may have heard about one of the oldest trees in the world, which was recently discovered — the Wollemi pine (SEE PaGE 84). If that gets you excited, then you're in the right place, especially if you take the Prehistoric Plant Tour at the garden. You might be surprised to learn which plants have been around for hundreds, or even thousands, of years!

UBC Botanical Garden has been around for almost a hundred years itself. Over that time, it has collected more than 8,000 different kinds of plants from all over the world, including Chile, China, France, Japan, and South Africa, not to mention all the plants from British Columbia and the rest of Canada. The garden is organized into several 'gardens', each with a particular focus, based on use or geographic origin.

Look up and you'll be in awe of how high the trees reach. Plus, you might notice something else way up there… It's the Greenheart Canopy Walkway — a suspension bridge in the forest canopy. The walkway lets you get an up-close look at the highest branches of the trees, and also allows you a glimpse of things you might not see from down on the ground, like mosses, lichens, birds, insects, and other invertebrates.

The Nitobe Memorial Garden is a traditional Japanese garden on the University of British Columbia (UBC) campus. This minimalist Zen garden has been carefully designed to symbolize a journey through life, with various symbols that represent life stages or events. For example, the stone lanterns represent choices in life, while bridges represent different life stages such as marriage. A map will walk you through the garden and all its symbols and meanings.

The Greenheart Canopy Walkway is over 300 metres (1,000 feet) long and reaches heights of 17.5 metres (57 feet).

When the Crown Prince (now Emperor) of Japan walked through the Nitobe Memorial Garden, his reaction was to say: "I am in Japan".

maKE a NEW (fiSHy) FRiENd

With more than 70,000 creatures, the Vancouver Aquarium is the biggest in Canada. There are 'local residents' from the British Columbian coast such as the giant Pacific octopus, wolf eels, and sunflower stars; tropical fish like sharks, damselfish, and seahorses; and typical Amazonian animals like crocodiles, fresh-water fish, and even exotic birds. There's also an impressive gallery featuring different kinds of jellyfish and a new 'Frogs Forever?' exhibit. In this exhibit, you'll learn about how a lot of frogs living in the wild are facing possible extinction, and you'll get a chance to see some of the frogs, toads, and salamanders the aquarium breeds and cares for.

But the absolute coolest thing about the aquarium is Animal Encounters. This is your chance to make friends with one of the aquarium's popular animals. You can choose a dolphin, a beluga whale, a sea turtle, a sea lion, or a sea otter. Your once-in-a-lifetime adventure begins when you meet up with an interpreter. They'll teach you all about the animal's habits and how it lives. Next, you'll stop off in the marine mammal kitchen, where you'll help to whip up a snack for your new animal friend. Finally, you'll head over to the animal's habitat. You might even be able to touch the animal or to participate in a full, interactive training session. It's definitely a wonderful, one-of-a-kind — not to mention wet — experience!!! You won't want to miss it.

cool, yEaH?

Do you know what the plural of octopus is? Don't worry! Nobody does for sure! It could be either octopuses, octopi, or even octopodes!!!

GET a FRESH PERSPECTIVE ON ART

The Vancouver Art Gallery is the biggest art gallery in British Columbia, with works by local, Canadian, and international artists. It's also home to the largest Emily Carr collection anywhere. Emily Carr, who lived in Victoria, British Columbia, is one of Canada's most beloved and acclaimed artists. She was very interested in First Nations' art and the intricate carvings on totem poles, as well as in the rain forests of Vancouver Island — both of which became the focus of a lot of the work she's best known for. Her art was also greatly influenced by the Group of Seven, a famous group of Canadian artists. She was especially inspired by Lawren Harris, who was a painter in the group.

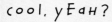

cool, yEaH?

Don't expect the art to end when you walk out the door. Several of the gallery's works are displayed outside. Can you spot them?

Today the emphasis is on Canadian works, but when the gallery first opened there were only seven works by Canadian artists (and six of those had been gifts)!

The weekends are a great time to visit the gallery. That's when a lot of cool activities for kids and families are offered. But the absolute best day to explore the gallery is Saturday, when Art Agents are on hand to explain things to you. You could also join a tour geared toward kids and led by artists, teachers, musicians, and scientists — a really mixed crowd! Are you wondering what scientists even have to do with art? Find out during Art Tracks. You'll never think about art the same way again! And if you'd rather make art than look at it, then you're also in luck. The Making Place offers creative hands-on workshops every second and fourth Sunday of the month, including painting and weaving, combined with reading, singing, and playing.

you can't top these vancouverized views!

Like many large cities, Vancouver has a tower that gives you a 360-degree view of the city and its surroundings. One of the special things about the Vancouver Lookout, however, is the variety of stuff you can see from the top: the city's downtown and its impressive architecture, the suburbs, the harbours and the docks (including Port Metro Vancouver), venues for the 2010 Winter Olympics, the North Shore Mountains, and all the way out to the Pacific Ocean.

You'll find the lookout on top of the Harbour Centre, perched at its very edge. Glass elevators take you on a 40-second ride, up 130 metres (430 feet) to the Observation Deck. Sure, it's not the tallest tower in Canada (not even close, actually) but you can't top the views!

It's no coincidence, either, that the city you see from up there is such a special place. As the city has developed, a hands-on planning style was used, known as **Vancouverism**, which places commercial and residential buildings in a single spot. Because the views are one of the highlights of the city, Vancouverism aims to protect the view corridors and to prevent blocking sightlines to the mountains to the north. To accomplish this, buildings are usually designed with shops, stores, or office space at the bottom and very narrow, residential high-rises on top that can hold lots of people. The result is a city with tall, narrow towers separated by low- and medium-rise buildings, public spaces, and parks. In this way, plenty of people can live in the city without the view of the surrounding area being lost. It's worked so well that other cities around the world are now 'Vancouverizing' themselves. And why not? This style of urban planning has helped the city to remain one of the most livable in the world.

cool, yEaH?

The tower stands at 177 metres (581 feet), but the deck is lower, at 130 metres (430 feet).

The Vancouver Lookout was officially opened in 1977 by astronaut Neil Armstrong, the first man to walk on the moon!

iMagiNE youRSElf sailiNG tHE SEas oN St Roch

In the late 15th century, explorers from Europe knew of only two ways to reach Asia by ship: (1) head east by rounding the southern tip of Africa or (2) head south-west and round the southern tip of South America. Both routes were long, with rough waters. Plus, Pope Alexander VI had split the discovered world (and, also, the two known routes), between Spain and Portugal. So other countries like France, England, and Holland were left without a way to get there. The search for the legendary Northwest Passage began.

For centuries, explorers searched for this passage, but it wasn't until 1906 that someone finally found it. Roald Amundsen, a Norwegian explorer, crossed the passage on his vessel, *Gjøa*, on a three-year journey travelling from east to west. But it wasn't until 1940 that the passage was crossed again, this time by Canadian RCMP officer Henry Larson, on the ship *St Roch*. His journey started in Vancouver and ended in Halifax, making it the first expedition to make it through the passage from west to east. *St Roch* also accomplished a few other 'firsts'. Not only was she the first ship to cross the passage in both directions, she was also the first ship to circumnavigate North America via the Panama Canal.

St Roch was an ice-fortified schooner that was initially used to patrol and carry supplies to the Canadian Arctic. After her return trip, she continued to patrol the Arctic. Eventually she came home to Vancouver to be preserved at the Vancouver Maritime Museum. Today, the ship is the pride and joy of the museum. In addition to *St Roch*, the museum has the *Ben Franklin* (NASA's undersea research vessel), a model ship collection and workshop, a children's maritime discovery centre, a collection of maritime art, and a library.

cool, yEaH?

Why do we keep calling St Roch 'she'? Traditionally, ships have been classified as feminine. It goes back to Ancient Greece, but the specific explanation is still a mystery.

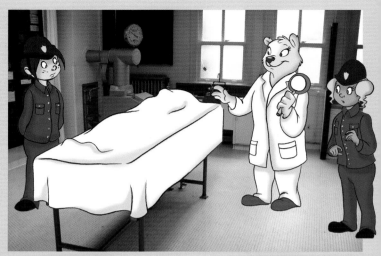

cool, yEaH?

The first thing police do at a crime scene is secure the perimeter. They have to be careful that nothing leaves or enters the scene, since that would cause contamination. Then any victims, witnesses, and suspects must be interviewed. The scene is then examined with a 'walk-through' that may give investigators an idea of what happened. Next, the area is photographed before evidence is carefully collected and packaged.

it'd bE cRiMiNal to miss this

The city of Vancouver celebrated its centennial (100th birthday) in 1986 with Expo 86. And so did the Vancouver Police Department! To commemorate this milestone, the Vancouver Police Museum was opened. The museum is in the same building that was once used as the Coroner's Court (where autopsies were performed) and the City Analyst's Laboratory (sort of a CSI lab back in the day). Some of the city's most infamous crimes were investigated here.

As you make your way through the museum, you'll see interesting artifacts, learn about policing methods and equipment from the past, see classic police vehicles and get the chance to look at several collections such as unusual guns, rare weapons, and counterfeit money. Many of these would have been collected during a crime scene investigation. You'll even have a chance to try on a real police uniform. Do you think you've got what it takes to become a police officer? Before you say 'yes', read on…

The creepy bit is in the back of the museum. First, there's the morgue. Once upon a time, behind those metal doors the bodies of victims were kept. You probably wouldn't have wanted to be there alone at night! And if you go a bit farther, you'll find yourself right in the middle of an actual autopsy room! If you get grossed out easily, don't get too close to the walls – samples of real body parts are all over them.

JUNIOR CREEPY ALERT! JETSETTERS

book some time for a visit

We know. You're probably thinking, "Why would anyone want to visit a library while they're on vacation?" But this isn't just any library we're talking about – it's the Vancouver Public Library's Central Branch, and it's like nothing you've ever seen before!

From the outside, the library's curving walls make it look like the ancient Colosseum in Rome, Italy. (Of course, it's not nearly as old.) Once you're inside, you'll see that the library is actually shaped like a rectangular block in the centre. The curved outer walls contain reading and study areas, and are connected to the centre block by bridges. One section of the wall curves farther out and creates a public area for the library's entrance. It also has several shops and restaurants – the perfect place to take a break when you're done being bookish.

Your favourite part, though, will definitely be the entire floor just for kids! Everything here has been designed and picked with you in mind – the books, the art, the furniture, and even the lounge. There are so many books, it'll make your head spin. They've also got computers, games, newspapers, magazines, encyclopædias, and comics. So grab a story or two, hop on a bean bag chair, and settle in for a great read.

cool, yEaH?

Moshe Safdie, the library's architect, also designed the National Gallery of Canada in Ottawa, the Yad Vashem Memorial in Jerusalem, the United States Institute of Peace in Washington, D.C., and several airports all over the world.

The library has a large selection of Canadian, French, picture, folk, and fairy tale books. All in all, the Children's Library has more than 80,000 books!

a GREEN GEt-away aNd a GREat placE to play

Like many areas of Vancouver and British Columbia, the site of the VanDusen Botanical Garden was once owned by the Canadian Pacific Railway. Until 1960, a golf club leased the land from the Railway. In 1966, to stop the site from being turned into a condominium development, it was bought by the Vancouver Park Board with funding from the city, the provincial government, the Vancouver Foundation, and a donation by W.J. VanDusen.

The VanDusen Botanical Garden is like a museum, but everything you'll see in it is alive, growing, and changing! The garden is also constantly adding plants to its collection. If you look up, you'll likely catch a glimpse of one of the 60 types of birds living here. Listen hard and you can hear the buzzing of the honey bees that make their home in the Garden's beehives – if you want to try their honey, stop by the Garden Shop.

One of the newer plants in the Garden is the Wollemi Pine. It's a very rare plant that was around way back in the time of the dinosaurs! It was believed to be extinct until 1994 when a bushwalker happened upon it in Wollemi National Park in the Blue Mountains west of Sydney, Australia. The Wollemi Pine may be more than 1,000 years old – making it one of the oldest trees in the world!

The VanDusen Botanical Garden is a great place to get back to nature in a relaxing way. Take off your shoes and feel the grass on your bare feet, plan ahead and bring a picnic, or, for something a little more adventurous, stop by the maze and make your way through the labyrinth of cedars. There are just a couple of rules though: don't leave anything behind when you're done and don't feed any animals!

cool, yEaH?

> *The spot where the Wollemi Pine was found is a heavily-guarded secret. In the wild, there are less than 100 of these mature trees.*

Wollemi is an Aboriginal word that means 'look around you, keep your eyes open, and watch out'. Kind of a big mouthful for such a small word...

aRt thou REady foR SomE ENtERtaiNMENt?

'O Romeo, Romeo, wherefore art thou Romeo?
Deny thy father and refuse thy name;
Or, if thou wilt not, be but sworn my love
And I'll no longer be a Capulet.'

You've probably heard those words before. They were written by the greatest English writer ever — William Shakespeare. Shakespeare was a poet and playwright who lived over 400 years ago in England. He wrote 38 plays, 154 sonnets, and several other poems, including two really long ones! Almost everybody reads at least a few things he's written in school at some point.

All of his plays are famous, and have been performed over and over since he wrote them. The line above is from one of his earliest works, *Romeo and Juliet*. It's about two young 'star-cross'd lovers' whose families are involved in a feud. Romeo and Juliet love each other and want to get married, even though their families are enemies. The play is a tragic romance, which ends when... well, you'll just have to read it or see it yourself to find out!

Romeo and Juliet is just one of the plays you might see in Vanier Park during Bard on the Beach, an annual summer Shakespeare festival. There are four plays to choose from, and they change every year. But one thing that doesn't is the setting. The main tent is open, so you'll watch a great performance with a view of the mountains, the water, and the sky behind. If you don't understand every word, don't worry — Shakespeare wrote in Elizabethan English, which is slightly different from what we speak today. You'll get used to it! Before you know it, you'll be caught up in the drama and tragedy, sniffling along with the rest of the audience and asking your parents 'wherefore art the Kleenex?'

cool, yEah?

If you like to act and happen to be in Vancouver for the summer, sign up for one of the two-week Young Shakespearean Workshops. With the help of professional actors, you'll rehearse a short version of a Shakespeare play. Then it's your turn to put on a show!

Shakespeare is credited for introducing 3,000 words into the English language. Not bad for someone who didn't receive much education.

FEEl So pEacHy oN tHE bEacHiEs

Imagine leaving your house (or hotel), turning right and walking a few minutes to reach the hustle and bustle of a busy downtown street. Now imagine if you could turn left instead and, within the same amount of time, be at the beach. That's Vancouver! Considering how much water there is in and around the city, it's not surprising you don't have to go far to enjoy the sun and sand. The Vancouver area has at least a dozen public beaches, most of them on the English Bay side of the city – Stanley Park has two of them! Here are our three favourites:

English Bay Beach is in the downtown area. Often called First Beach, it's always full of people hanging out on the sand or the grassy area nearby. You can play volleyball, ride bikes or rollerblade along the Seawall, or kayak in English Bay. Join the locals here one evening and you'll be rewarded with an awesome sunset.

Kitsilano Beach is the hippest, most 'happening' beach. The locals call it Kits Beach. Like English Bay Beach, it's always busy: the tennis and basketball courts are always full, the playground is packed with kids, and the Oceanside saltwater heated outdoor pool is always popular. This beach probably has the best view (towards the city, Stanley Park, and the Coast Mountains) and is the ideal place to catch the HSBC Celebration of Light fireworks in summer.

Ambleside Beach in West Vancouver is the perfect place for having a picnic, swimming in the pool, sailboarding, flying a kite, playing a round of pitch and putt golf, or building sand castles. And for ship-lovers, this spot has the best view of cruise ships as they come and go from Vancouver.

cool, yEah?

Every January 1st, at 2:30 pm, members of the Vancouver Polar Bear Swim Club take a frosty plunge into English Bay. Families are invited — all you need to do is register before the swim to become club members.

cYcliNG RulEs + SafEty tips

1. *Always wear a helmet.*
2. *Learn and obey the rules of the road.*
3. *Pay attention to the signs.*
4. *Learn all biking symbols.*
5. *Do not ride on sidewalks unless allowed by signs.*
6. *Signal with your hands before turning.*
7. *Pay attention to what's around you.*
8. *Do not wear headphones while bicycling.*
9. *Make sure your bike has a working bell.*
10. *Always keep at least one hand on the handlebars.*
11. *Give buses the right of way.*
12. *Always lock your bike when you park.*

SEE tHE city oN two WHEEls

Vancouver has over 300 kilometres of bike paths and lanes, and more are being added all the time. You'll find them both on busy streets and in parks. The best and most popular place for a bike ride, though, is definitely on the Seawall (SEE paGE 66). The path extends 22 kilometres, starting near Canada Place, making its way around Stanley Park, False Creek, and Granville Island, and then ending just past Kitsilano. That's definitely a long enough ride, even for the most avid biker!

The city also has a huge network of Greenways. These are paths for walkers and cyclists that connect Vancouver's parks, nature reserves, cultural features, landmarks, historic sites, and neighbourhoods to each other. They're a safe and convenient way to get around and to see the city's natural environment.

For a chance to meet fellow cyclists, you can also join Critical Mass. This event, held on the last Friday of every month, is a chance for you and your parents to ditch the car and use only human-powered vehicles. Most participants do ride bikes, but skateboards, rollerblades, roller skates, and even walking shoes are welcome, too. Whatever locomotion means you choose, you'll be part of a marvelous, motor-less mass that makes its way through Vancouver.

cool, yEah?

TransLink, Vancouver's public transportation
company, operates the SeaBus service, which
uses two large catamarans to cross the Burrard
Inlet to North Vancouver every 15 to 30 minutes.

The TransLink vessels are named the
Burrard Beaver and the Burrard Otter.

take a tEENy-tiny taxi boat

In most cities, when you want to get from one place to another, you hop on a bus or subway, or hail a taxi. But what do you do when the city is surrounded on almost all sides by water? Sure, one option is to go all the way around the water until you reach your destination. But that can take a long time and can cost a lot if you're going by cab. It's also really annoying when you can see your destination right across the water! Obviously, boats are the answer!

Like a taxi on water, Vancouver's small ferries make their way back and forth to various spots on each side of the water and are an important mode of transportation in the city. The ferries to the south of downtown, in False Creek, have become vital and some might even say famous. They're great for visitors making their way to popular sights such as Granville Island (SEE paGE 20) or Science World (SEE paGE 22). But they're also used by Vancouverites who commute from one side of False Creek to the other. There are two main fleets: False Creek Ferries and Aquabus. They're easy to spot. False Creek's ferries are the little blue ones, while Aquabus's are rainbow-coloured. They'll likely be the most fun you'll ever have on public transit, plus, they've got the greatest views!

GEt REady to GO-GO-GO-kaRt!!!

You're probably at least a few years away from getting behind the wheel and going for a drive in a real car. So, while you wait, try out the next best thing: go-karts.

These tiny cars are nothing like the station wagon or minivan your parents might drive, though, and a go-kart track isn't a place where you'll drive slowly and learn the rules of the road. These 'cars' are purely for racing! If you've ever seen a Formula One race, such as a Grand Prix, then this will all look very familiar. Like a professional race car driver, you'll suit up with protective gear (racers always wear a helmet!), strap yourself in behind the wheel, and take off around a track full of twists and turns, curves, corners, and straightaways, while reaching speeds of 40-50 km/h! All the elements you need for a thrilling ride.

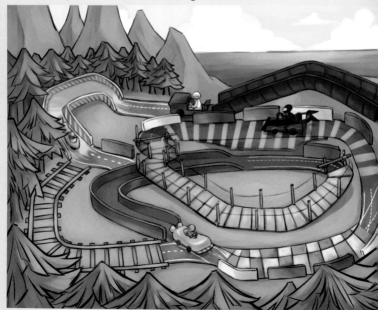

cool, yEah?

Superkarts (not the kind you'll find here) can reach speeds of 260 km/h! That's a bit too speedy for non-professionals, though...

a waterbound way to see the awesome scenery

So much of Vancouver is on the waterfront. So what better way to see the city and its sights than from the water? To the south of downtown you'll find False Creek. The small ferries here are perfect for sightseeing and getting around (SEE PaGE 92).

Burrard Inlet, a shallow extension of the Strait of Georgia lies between downtown Vancouver and the cities of North Vancouver and West Vancouver. The area around the Burrard Inlet was once home to several First Nations peoples (SEE PaGE 28). Spanish and British explorers were the first Europeans to discover the inlet, which British Captain George Vancouver named after his friend, Sir Harry Burrard-Neale.

The inlet's location, its calm waters, and its easy access to the open ocean made it the ideal location for a port, which eventually helped Vancouver become the city it is today. One of the highlights of the inlet, and something that you can't possibly miss, is Canada Place, a large pier/building with a sail-like roof (SEE PaGE 36). Canada Place is also the main cruise ship port of Vancouver. You'll also see some other major landmarks from a whole new perspective, such as Stanley Park and Lions Gate Bridge. On the other side you'll spot the North Shore Mountains, behind North Vancouver.

Other cruises take visitors farther east to Indian Arm (a body of water located within the Coast Mountains, which is almost completely inaccessible by car), or around English Bay on the other side of Stanley Park and downtown Vancouver.

cool, yEah?

Burrard Inlet is actually a fjord, which was formed during the last Ice Age. Fjords are made when glaciers cut a deep valley into the bedrock.

Row youR boat GENtly down thE stREam... oR iNlEt, oR cREEk, oR bay

There's a lot of water in and around Vancouver. (You might have noticed, right?) In fact, it's practically impossible to go anywhere in the city without a view of, and easy access to, water. Metro Vancouver is divided by a large body of water called Burrard Inlet. English Bay, Coal Harbour, and False Creek are some of the other bodies of water that you'll probably hear about and come across.

But all of this water isn't just nice to look at. It can also be a whole lot of fun. If you want to hang out on a beach, you can (SEE PaGE 88). If you want to cruise around on a boat or ferry, you can do that, too (SEE PaGE 92 + 96). If you like to do things rather than sit around and look at them, then you're definitely in luck. Instead of hopping on a sightseeing bus or boat, why not join a guided kayaking tour? You can enjoy the water, the scenery, and the cityscape while discovering the city in an adventurous, and healthy, way. After all, what could be better than exploring the area the way the First Nations people and early explorers did hundreds of years ago?

You'll be able to choose from many options in different areas of Vancouver. Your aquatic adventure will start with a dry introduction to kayaking. You'll also get all the gear you need to stay safe while you paddle around Granville Island or along the shorelines of Stanley Park, enjoying a view of the mountains and the city. If you'd rather enjoy the water surrounded by the British Columbian wild, you don't even have to go far. The many rivers near the city, especially to the north, provide a perfect spot for canoeing, kayaking and, for thrill seekers among you, river rafting!

cool, yEah?

First Nations people made their dug-out canoes from single trees. Sometimes, while working on a canoe, a flaw would be found and the whole canoe would be abandoned.

FORGET about SIGHTSEEING...
iN VANCOUVER you caN GO FLIGHTSEEING!

If you've walked along the Seawall near Canada Place (SEE PaGE 36) or the new Convention Centre, you've probably seen the seaplanes landing and taking off at Coal Harbour. But you might still be surprised to learn that Coal Harbour has an international airport (serving as a port of entry into Canada and staffed with Canada Border Service agents)! It's called the Coal Harbour Sea Plane Base. It doesn't look like any airport you've seen before, does it?

There are several airlines that fly from the Coal Harbour Sea Plane Base (often called the Vancouver Harbour Water Airport). These airlines' fleets consist of seaplanes, mainly floatplanes, which can take off and land on water. These planes (which are sometimes called hydroplanes), are perfect for touring the Vancouver area. The geography around the city is so diverse and there's no better way to see it than from up above. There are tons of tours to choose from: Whistler and the mountains beyond, the fjords and local villages of the Sunshine Coast north of Vancouver, the alpine lakes and glaciers of Mount Mamquam, Victoria and Vancouver Island, or the orcas of the Pacific Ocean. Whatever you decide, you're in for one amazing flightseeing adventure.

cool, yEaH?

> You probably don't see an airport control
> tower. That's because it's located on top of
> an office building nearby. It's the highest
> air traffic control tower in the world.

There are two types of seaplanes:
floatplanes and flying boats. Floatplanes
have pontoons under them that come into
contact with water. With flying boats, the
fuselage comes into contact with water. The
fuselage looks and acts like a boat's hull.

MuSiC FoR YouR FolKS
(PluS you MiGHt liKE it, too!)

Way, waaaaaay back in the 1970s when your parents were kids (or maybe even before they were born!) folk music started to become popular. Around the same time, Winnipeg in Manitoba was preparing to celebrate its centennial (100th birthday). Plans were made for a folk festival. It was supposed to be a one-time event, but it was so popular that it was held the next year, too. And it's been happening ever since. Its creator then decided that Vancouver would be a great place for a similar folk festival. And he was right!

The Vancouver Folk Music Festival is one of the city's most popular summer events. The weekend-long festival is held every July in Jericho Beach Park, right by one of the city's many beaches. When you hear the words folk music,

you might think of twanging guitars and humming harmonicas. But actually, folk music isn't one specific type of music at all. And it doesn't all sound the same. Folk music is popular traditional music from any country or region in the world — it could be a traditional tune, roots or revival music (an interpretation of folk music with modern dressing), or world music, a term that describes music of the world, often with common influences such as jazz.

The Vancouver Folk Music Festival is especially diverse. Tons of artists from North, Central, and South America; Africa; Europe; and Australia come together and play folk, roots, blues, Afro beats, hip hop, and more. You'll also have a chance to sample other traditions, cultures, and foods. In fact, you can pretty much experience the world without leaving the comfort of your picnic blanket or lounge chair.

cool, yEaH?

In its early years, the Vancouver Folk Music Festival also had its own recording label and distributor — Festival Records.

The Little Folks Village is an area with activities, special music, arts and crafts, and hands-on experiences that will immerse you in world culture.

oNE WEEK of KiddiNG aRouNd...

Imagine a week-long festival where everything is designed and planned just for you! The Vancouver International Children's Festival — held in Vanier Park — is all about shows and activities for kids. There's theatre, music, dance, circus and variety acts, puppets, stories, and more. In a single day you could listen to a First Nations artist tell stories revealed in a totem pole, then learn American Sign Language (ASL) to discover the culture of the deaf and deaf-blind, make and then fly your own kite, find out what cool things you can make from recyclable materials like aluminum, get an airbrush tattoo, and live like the First Nations people did in a real teepee village. The list goes on and on. If only the day was longer (and you didn't have a bedtime)...

Two days of the festival are dedicated to French-language shows and activities. Known as Les Journées FrancoFun, these days help promote and celebrate Canada's other official language. How do you say 'Fun' *en français*? Find out here! But don't worry if you don't speak French — there are English-language activities available on these days, too!

There's also tons of stuff to discover in the park itself, which is a bit of an outdoor museum. Works of art are located all over, including the giant steel crab fountain in front of the Space Centre, the *Discus Thrower* behind it, and the extremely tall totem pole near the Maritime Museum. Other Annual festivals held here include the Pacific Rim Kite Festival and Bard on the Beach (SEE PaGE 86).

cool, yEah?

The Vancouver International Children's Festival was the first of its kind. Today, there are similar festivals in New York and Boston, as well as in cities across Europe and the rest of the world.

slidE. SplaSH. SWiM. REPEat

Rivers, rapids, valleys, canyons, coves, parks... We're not talking about the natural features of Vancouver and British Columbia, although the area has plenty of those. We're talking about the attractions you'll come across in some of the many water parks around Vancouver. Of course, you'll also find water slides of all sizes and types, tube rides, pools, hot tubs, and playgrounds... Basically, if you can imagine it, chances are you'll find it!

Water parks, like Bridal Falls and Cultus Lake, provide adventures and thrills for everyone, including that younger brother or sister of yours who's tagging along but who can't yet enjoy British Columbia's real rivers, lakes, and other water activities. A trip to one of these parks is also a great way to relax after a few busy days of sightseeing, biking, walking, and hiking in Vancouver.

cool, yEaH?

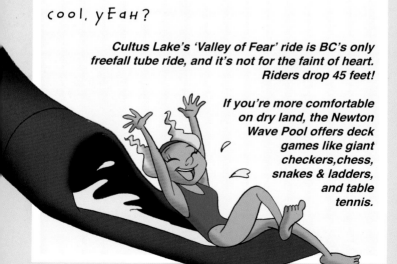

Cultus Lake's 'Valley of Fear' ride is BC's only freefall tube ride, and it's not for the faint of heart. Riders drop 45 feet!

If you're more comfortable on dry land, the Newton Wave Pool offers deck games like giant checkers, chess, snakes & ladders, and table tennis.

Of course, if you prefer an amusement park for relaxing, then Playland (SEE PaGE 60) is a great place for you. But, honestly, on those sizzling hot days is there anything better than racing down a winding slide and splashing into a cool pool?

find out what's up underground

With all the forests around B.C., you probably won't be surprised to hear that forestry is the province's biggest and most important natural resource. But what you might not know is that mining used to be an important industry here, too. In 1888, copper was discovered at Britannia Mountain.

Eventually, British Columbia became the largest copper producer in the British Commonwealth (the international community of countries that were formerly British colonies). But the construction of a railway, followed by the Squamish highway, had an unexpected effect on the mine, as did low copper prices. Workers started to leave the area, heading for the city, until only seven employees remained. The mine was sold and the new owners finally closed it in 1974. Ever since, it's been the BC Museum of Mining.

A visit to the museum is your chance to learn about fossils, minerals, and mineshafts. You can even try panning for gold. And guess what? Whatever you find, you actually get to keep! You'll also see some of the old mining equipment, including a 235-tonne Super Truck (if you have no idea how large a 235-tonne truck is, wait and see...) and the gravity-fed concentrator mill, which separates the copper or other mineral from rock. But that's not the best part. When you hear the train bell, grab a hardhat and climb aboard. You'll go on a ride underground through the authentic, old mining tunnel.

Note: *Make sure to follow all safety rules. Hardhats must be worn in the tunnel. And it's best if you wear closed-toed/covered shoes. It does get cold underground, so bring a sweater.*

tHE coNcENtRatiNG pRocEss

(1) **Crushing & Grinding Ore** – *The rock (or 'ore') is crushed and ground several times by different machines. The result is ore that feels like sugar or salt. This is called 'fines'.* *(2)* **Flotation** – *Water and other chemicals are added to the fines in large pools (called 'cells'). This forms a thick soupy mixture called 'slurry'. The combination of air and chemicals causes the mineral to rise to the surface to be collected.* *(3)* **Dewatering (Thickening)** – *The minerals are still in a watery mixture at this stage. Machines agitate the mixture, causing the mineral to settle to the bottom. It is then filtered and dried, becoming 'concentrate'.*

cool, yEah?

*Buddha is not, and never was, a god.
A Buddha is a human being who has awakened
and sees things as they really are.*

*Everyone has the potential to become a
Buddha (if they study and meditate a lot).*

aRE you a buddiNG buddHist?

Buddhism is a philosophy and a way of life based on the teachings, beliefs, and practices of Prince Siddhartha Gautama. Siddhartha Gautama is usually known as the *Buddha* (Sanskrit language for 'Awakened One'). Prince Siddhartha Gautama was born in what is now the Kingdom of Nepal, in Asia. One day, he left his palace and for the first time saw sick, elderly, and dying people in the streets. He travelled the world to understand the true meaning of suffering and to find a way to relieve people of it. It took him six years to find the answers and to attain Enlightenment, in the process becoming the Buddha.

Buddhism encourages people to lead a moral life; to be aware of their thoughts and actions; and to develop wisdom, understanding, and compassion for all living things. Buddhism originated over 2,600 years ago and was practised mostly in India. Over time, it spread and is now practised all over the world. Although the emphasis changes, the point of the teaching doesn't – the *Dhamma* (or truth).

One type of Buddhism is Mahayana, which is the most-practised type in China. The Buddhist Temple was built to provide Buddhists in and around Vancouver with an authentic Chinese temple in which to study and practise Chinese Mahayana Buddhism. The temple, the largest in Canada, is an amazing example of traditional Chinese architecture and is modelled after the Forbidden City in Beijing. It's surrounded by a forest and a classical Chinese garden.

Important Note: *The temple is a place for meditation. Please respect other visitors. Speak quietly and stay calm while you're on the grounds.*

gEt a littlE tastE of 'back iN tHE day...'

"Back when I was a child…" Have you ever heard your grandparents or great-grandparents start a story like that? Here's your chance to find out if what they were telling you was 100 per cent true, or if they were just exaggerating to make a point.

Burnaby Village Museum is a real village from the 1920s. In the 1890s, the BC Electric Railway was being built from Vancouver to New Westminster. One of the stops for this Interurban tram was Burnaby. It wasn't long before a small village developed here, as well as at other stops on the line.

cool, yEaH?

The Carousel's maker, Mr. C.W. Parker called it a 'Carry-Us-All' rather than a 'Merry-Go-Round'.

The Interurban tram #1223 was recently fully restored. It was completely taken apart, leaving only the floor and the roof. The rest was carefully restored or recreated and placed back exactly the way it was in 1913.

The village you'll see here today combines original buildings as well as some replica and rebuilt ones. You can tour typical homes, or stop by shops such as a drugstore, a barbershop, a general store, a post office, a bakery, a blacksmith, an optometrist, a schoolhouse, a bank, and a church. There's even a movie theatre — but don't expect to see the latest new release. Back then, there were only black and white movies.

As you tour the streets, you'll get a real sense of what day-to-day life was like back then. For instance, you can watch a blacksmith bend red-hot metal, visit a Chinese herbalist who may recommend some interesting and unusual cures for your aches and pains, or check out the Interurban tram #1223, that once ran through the village. And definitely don't leave without taking a spin on the old local Carousel.

. _ _ . ._ . . ._ . ._ ._ . .._ _ _ _ ._ .
. ._ .. .. .._ . _ _ _ _ .._ . .._.

Do you like visiting airports and watching the planes take off and land above your head? Do you like looking at planes up close? Old ones, new ones, big ones, little ones? Then it sounds like you're a true 'Junior Jetsetter'! Grab your parents and head out of the city to Langley, where you'll find the Canadian Museum of Flight.

The museum is in one of Langley Airport's hangars, which is pretty appropriate for an airplane museum! If you're lucky, while you're there, you might see some planes coming in for a landing. You'll also see dozens of old, restored aircraft and will learn about the vital role some of these planes played during the First and Second World Wars.

The restoration of planes at the museum is done on-site by volunteers and can take months, or even years. The museum's 1937 Waco AQC Cabin biplane took 22 years to bring back to flying condition! After all, some of these planes are really old, so it's not as if you can buy replacement parts in a shop. They have to be found, salvaged, or even made from scratch! Many of the museum's planes don't fly anymore, but there are seven that do, including the Waco AQC. Another working airplane you'll see is the Harvard which, in 2009, participated in a round-trip cross-country relay by vintage aircraft to celebrate the 100th anniversary of powered flight in Canada.

Before leaving, check out the Millennium Kids Room. Here you'll find displays that you can touch. You'll learn about the forces of flight — how propellers and fins work with the air and wind — and you'll even see the inside of an engine and learn what makes it work.

cool, yEah?

The only displayed Handley Page Hampden plane in the world is at the Canadian Museum of Flight.

The museum's website has everything you ever wanted to know about its plane collection, including each aircraft's history, uses, speed, and other data.

Use the Morse Code chart in the museum to decipher the dots and dashes at the top.

a REal, aNd REally RuGGEd, wildERNESS ExpERiENcE

Before Europeans settled in British Columbia, three groups of First Nations peoples lived in what we now call Cape Scott National Park: the *T'łat'łasik'wala* (Tlatlasikwala), the *Nəqəmgəlisəla* (Nakumgilisala) and the *Yúx̌inux̌ʷ* (Yutlinuk). Today some of these peoples remain in the area and are collectively known as the Nahwitti. It was the First Nations peoples who created early trails through the area that includes the park, using them for trade, to harvest resources, and to visit locations they considered sacred.

In the early 1900s, there were two settlement attempts by Europeans in the area, but neither one lasted long. Still, some artifacts from these times can be seen in the park, including a three-metre-tall granite tombstone, several corduroy roads, many ruins that look like mossy mounds, and some rusty farming equipment.

116

These days, the park is known for its old growth forest and sandy beaches, and is a favourite spot for backpackers, especially in the summer. It's not for everyone, though. The park is secluded, the terrain is rugged and the area is known for its heavy rain and violent storms. To get there, you drive down a logging road in the south, but the rest of it is accessible only by foot, helicopter, or boat. A popular backpacking trip is the 16.8-km Cape Scott Trail to Nels Bight hike, which usually takes 4–7 hours each way and is rated as easy/moderate, making it a good fit for fit kids! It's mostly flat, but often very muddy, so bring along a hiking stick to measure the depth of bogs and mud pits before stepping in! Or if you're looking for a shorter trail, check out the path to the beach at San Josef Bay.

Even though a lot of the park trails have wooden boardwalks, the 43.1-km North Coast Trail, opened in 2008, is an extension to the Cape Scott Trail with some very difficult sections! In fact, the park authority has extensive warnings for all visitors about what gear to take and how to use the park site. You should check the website before visiting, and keep in mind that this is a wilderness site with many potential dangers… including bears and cougars!

cool, yEaH?

Be cautious when travelling along Cape Scott's trails. If you see a bear, let it know you're there by talking as loudly as possible. If the bear continues to walk towards you, back up and get well off the trail to let the bear pass you. And always remember to keep pets on a leash! Not even your large dog is a match for this mighty predator.

JUNIOR
FAR AWAY
JETSETTERS

stRap oN youR skis aNd sliiiiide

With so many mountains around Vancouver, it's easy to see why the city was picked for the 2010 Olympic and Paralympic Winter Games. The fact that the city itself gets very little snow doesn't affect the skiing in the nearby mountains, which are covered in snow during the winter.

There are three main skiing spots within a short drive from Vancouver: Grouse Mountain (SEE PaGE 50), Cypress Mountain, and Mount Seymour. Over the years, these areas have expanded to include much more than skiing. So if alpine (downhill) skiing isn't your thing, don't worry. And if you've never tried it before, here's your chance — all three places offer ski rentals and beginner lessons.

The Cypress Mountain resort, in West Vancouver, offers alpine skiing, nordic (cross-country) skiing, snowboarding, snowtubing, and snowshoeing in the winter, and a bike park and plenty of hiking trails in the summer. There are several mountains on the resort (Mount Strachan, Black Mountain, and Hollyburn Mountain), with 52 ski runs. Cypress Mountain was chosen as the official freestyle skiing and snowboarding venue for the 2010 Olympic Games.

Mount Seymour is an actual mountain located in Mount Seymour Provincial Park in North Vancouver. It is a smaller resort with 23 ski runs and trails. Snowboarding, snowtubing, and snowshoeing are also available. The resort even offers a hill with eight runs just for tobogganing, so get ready to slide (and remember to keep your fingers inside)!

cool, yEaH?

Toboggans were originally used by the Indigenous peoples of northern Canada. They're different from other sleds in that they ride directly on the snow. There are no runners underneath.

Cypress Mountain and Mount Seymour get about 1,000 centimetres of snow a year. That's 10 metres — about the same height as a three-storey house!

discoVER tHE pRoud hERitaGE of fiRSt NatioNS pEoplES

People were living in what is now British Columbia for thousands of years before the first Europeans arrived. Although the area around Vancouver was an ideal place for these early inhabitants, it wasn't the only place they lived. The mild climate and wealth of natural resources of the Northwest Coast led to the development of many Aboriginal cultures and peoples who have always shared a close connection to the land and the environment.

Although many groups (or nations) shared similarities, each developed its own history, culture, and way of life. Location played a big part in this. For example, the Haida lived (and continue to live) on Haida Gwaii (Queen Charlotte Island), an island off the northwest coast. Being surrounded by water, they became master canoe builders and water warriors.

Some of the First Nations that lived around Vancouver include: *K'ómoks* (Comox), *Stó:lō* (Sto:lo), Tsawwassen, *Kwikwetlem* (Coquitlam), Okanagan, Quw'utsun', Gitxsan, *Kwakwaka'wakw* (Kwakkewith), *Xat'súll* (Xats'ull or Soda Creek), *Dakelhne* (Carrier), and *Tsek'ehne* (Sekani). You might recognize some of these names – they've become the names of many cities and towns in British Columbia.

Today there are 198 First Nations communities in British Columbia. The Elders pass along their traditions, songs, dances, and customs to the younger members to ensure their cultures live on, the way they have been doing for thousands of years. Proud of their heritage, many First Nations peoples have opened cultural centres and traditional villages for anyone who wishes to learn more about their culture and ways of life. Here's your chance to hear ancient stories, taste traditional foods and even find out what happened during a potlatch. (Hint: it has nothing to do with a potluck!)

cool, yEah?

Sekani people call themselves Tsek'ehne or Tθek'ehne, *meaning 'People on the Rocks'. Their language is called* tse'khene.

Even though Indigenous peoples have been known by different names in the past (such as Natives, Indians, and American Indians), First Nations is the preferred name today. You'll also hear Aboriginal peoples occasionally.

121

tHE oldEst sHopping cEntRE you'RE likEly to sEE!

It's weird to think that, what today is a Canadian department store, once played a huge role in the discovery of western Canada — but it did! The Hudson's Bay Company controlled the fur trade in much of British-controlled North America for centuries, exploring the land as they traded. The company set up a network of trading posts all over the northern part of the continent, and Fort Langley was one of them.

The Fort was built in 1827 on the Fraser River, in the middle of a large Aboriginal population. However, the Fort's trading partners weren't limited to this population and it turned out that furs weren't the only item of importance. Furs were shipped to Europe, produce was traded to the Russians in Alaska (Alaska wasn't a U.S. state back then), cranberries were traded to the Americans in California, and salmon — a lot of it — made it all the way to Hawaii.

In 1858, because of rumours of gold in the Fraser River, a huge number of Americans arrived, setting up camp right outside Fort Langley. Worried that they would be taken over by the Americans, the inhabitants sent word to England, asking for help. In November of that year, Queen Victoria proclaimed the area a Crown Colony named British Columbia. Fort Langley and the Hudson's Bay Company soon became a thriving retail business. Over the next three decades, however, business decreased (the gold rush had ended) and the fort declined. By 1886, it was no longer a company post.

Today, the site consists of original and reconstructed buildings, including the Big House, the Servants' Quarters, the Depot, the Storehouse (the oldest building, maybe even in all of British Columbia!), the Blacksmith Shop, and the Cooperage (where barrels were built for all that salmon).

cool, yEaH?

The name suggests that Fort Langley was a military fort. It wasn't — no fighting ever took place here. It was strictly for trading.

Chinook Jargon, a unique mix of English and Aboriginal languages, developed in the area. It was used between the European traders and the First Nations peoples.

cool, yEaH?

Zoo officials have learned that lions and tigers should have a day when they don't eat. So this zoo's wild cats have a meal break on Wednesdays.

You can even spend a night in the wild at the zoo — camping under the stars and listening to the lions roar, the wolves howl, and the baboons yell.

ZOOM tHROUGH tHE ZOO by biKE oR oN RollERbladEs

Everyone knows that lions and bears roar, wolves howl and elephants trumpet, but what do *capybaras*, *ibex*, *kulans*, or *guanacos* say? What do they even look like? No idea? Well, when you visit the Greater Vancouver Zoo, you're likely to find out.

You'll also learn about several animals kept at the zoo that are now considered to be critically endangered. They include the Père David's Deer and the Siberian Tiger. The Greater Vancouver Zoo, like many zoos all over the world, is putting a huge emphasis on conservation. The goal of conservation is to protect animals, their habitats, and ecosystems and to prevent them from becoming extinct. A big part of this involves studying the animals, which the zoo does, and learning all about them, like you'll do there.

But it's not all serious at the zoo. It's definitely a place for you to have fun. Grab your bike or rollerblades and zoom around the park! Yep, you read correctly — you're actually encouraged to bike or rollerblade through the zoo! The Quadra-Cycles are another option, but you'll need three cycling partners. If you want to relax and let someone else do all the driving, book a ride on the Safari Express, a narrated train tour. Or hop on the North American Wilds bus tour, which takes you into the enclosures, letting you get up close and personal with the bears, wolves, bison, and elk. And, of course, you won't want to miss the lion, tiger, and baboon feedings.

lEaRN HoW to caN a SalMoN iN SiX Easy StEpS!

The West Coast's fishing industry dates back to when First Nations people established settlements along the coast. They fished for herring, cod, sole, halibut, and salmon. During the 1800s, foreigners began to arrive. They included European, Chinese, and Japanese migrants who, along with the First Nations peoples, harvested the fish.

In 1870, commercial fishing began on the West Coast when the first canning factory opened. Many more canneries soon followed. At one time there were over 60 of them! The most important fishing village was Steveston (SEE PaGE 134), which had at least 15 canneries. The Gulf of Georgia Cannery, which you can visit today, is pretty typical of one of these canneries. It was built in 1894 and produced canned salmon until the 1930s.

Want to know how to can a salmon? There are several steps involved, and back when the cannery opened, they were all done by hand—talk about a slimy job! Thankfully, over time, machines automated the process.

Here's how you do it:

Step 1: Butcher the salmon. Cut the belly open and take out the guts. Remove the head, tail, and fins.
Step 2: Clean the salmon and make sure it was properly butchered.
Step 3: Cut the salmon into pieces, which must fit into the can.
Step 4: Fill the can with salmon pieces and add salt for flavour.
Step 5: Put the lid on the can, remove the air to make a vacuum, and seal the can tightly.
Step 6: Cook the can of salmon for 80 minutes. (Watch out! If all the air was not removed during Step 5, the can will explode during Step 6!)

cool, yEah?

The Gulf of Georgia Cannery was the largest cannery in British Columbia until 1902. It was known as the 'Monster Cannery'. In 1897 it packed over 2.5 million cans of salmon!

Almost all the canned salmon produced was sent to England since it was a cheap source of protein.

take a (Not-so-terrifying) tRam Ride to Hell's Gate

The roar of the river, the rush of the rapids, the pressure of the water as it passes through a narrow canyon… this is Hell's Gate, on the Fraser River. The Fraser River is the longest river in British Columbia and is named after Simon Fraser, who fully explored it in 1808. It starts way up in the Rockies (SEE PaGE 132) and empties into the Strait of Georgia.

Parts of the river are calm and still, while others can be really treacherous. A particularly dangerous area in the Fraser Canyon has earned the name, Hell's Gate. Simon Fraser described this narrow section of the river as an "awesome gorge" and said that "surely we have encountered the gates of hell". You can probably image that it's a pretty cool sight, from a safe distance, anyway.

Is a spot 150 metres above it safe enough for you? We think so! So get on board the Hell's Gate Airtram for a bird's eye view of the gorge from the safety of the red gondola. And when you're done that, check out the suspension bridge across the canyon or the several observation decks that provide amazing views of the Fraser River and Hell's Gate. If you didn't get to Fort Langley (SEE PaGE 122) to pan for gold, you'll have your chance here. Sift through gravel from Hill's Bar on the Fraser River — the same area where the biggest claim was staked in the Fraser Canyon in the 1860s. A salmon exhibit and a fudge factory will complete your visit.

cool, yEaH?

The construction of the Canadian Northern Railway damaged the sockeye salmon run. To repair the damage, fishways ('highways' for fish) were built along the gorge to help millions of salmon reach their spawning grounds.

COME SEE THE SEa

Even though, technically, Vancouver is bathed by the Pacific Ocean, you can't see the open sea from the city. To catch a glimpse, you have to head out west to Vancouver Island's southwestern coast. Here, you'll find Pacific Rim National Park. Established in the 1970s as a national park reserve, the area is famous for its magnificent islands, beautiful beaches, and dramatic seascapes. It's also known for a place everyone calls the 'lake', which is actually a saltwater fjord often listed as one of the top ten windsurfing spots in the world! The park is subject to moist air masses, and lots of rain, creating some of the temperate rainforests British Columbia is famous for. It is divided into three different geographic areas, all of which are scattered with campsites in stunning locations where you can rest with your family and be marvelled by nature.

Long Beach, the most accessible area for visitors, goes from Tofino to Ucluelet, and is basically a long sandy beach with bogs and rainforests along the way. Because this is where Captain James Cook first arrived in 1778, it's also a historically significant site.

The Broken Group Islands are made up of about 100 islands and islets in Barkley Sound. Unfortunately — or fortunately — they can only be reached by boat, which has made them extremely popular with kayakers. If you and your family are planning to camp there, make sure you take all the water you need for your stay since there's no drinking water available.

The 72-km West Coast Trail is the third section, and the highlight of the park, going from Renfrew to Bamfield. It was originally built as a base for launching rescue operations at sea in the early 20th century. When it was turned into a park in the 1970s, the trail became an instant paradise for hikers, who love the rocky beaches, the thick, soggy rainforests, and even the rough and muddy terrain. It's beautiful, but also a long hike. You can walk the trail comfortably in 5–7 days, but you do need to be somewhat experienced in the wild.

cool, yEaH?

To make a rainforest, you need lots of rain, snow, drizzle, mist, and fog — a minimum 250 cm of moisture (100 inches) per year. The maritime landscape at the Pacific Rim is wet most of the year, with precipitation reaching 300 inches.

The arrival of large numbers of grey whales to the park is celebrated every spring in the Pacific Rim Whale Festival. You can also spot seals and sea lions, as well as over 330 species of birds!

mouNtaiNs tHat (litERally) Rock

Everyone has heard of the Rocky Mountains — the huge range of mountains that stretches from northern British Columbia to New Mexico. But they aren't the only mountains in B.C. Farther west, closer to the Pacific Ocean, lie the Pacific Coast Ranges (called the Pacific Mountain System in the United States). The mountains you see in Vancouver are the North Shore Mountains, located in a section of the Pacific Coast Ranges called the Coast Mountains. Whistler (SEE paGE 144) is in the Coast Mountains. To reach the Rockies, you have to go farther east, toward Alberta. But to really experience these magnificent mountains, head to Jasper or Banff National Parks. It's a full day's drive from Vancouver, and it might be hard to convince your mom and dad to do it, but it's definitely worth trying!

Banff National Park is the oldest national park in the Rockies. It has several glaciers, ice fields, thick forests

JUNIOR FAR AWAY JETSETTERS

cool, yEaH?

There are five national parks in the Canadian Rockies — Banff, Jasper, Kootenay, Waterton Lakes, and Yoho. The five parks together are a UNESCO World Heritage Site, which means they are a treasure for all of mankind.

The Icefields Parkway that connects Lake Louise (in Banff National Park) and Jasper is one of the most scenic highways in the world!

and, of course, mountains. There are activities here all year round. During the summer there's golfing, horseback riding, camping, climbing, and hiking. In the winter, the main attractions are the ski resorts.

Jasper National Park is the largest national park in the Rocky Mountains and is located north of Banff National Park. It's full of glaciers, hot springs, lakes, waterfalls, and mountains. This park offers hiking, fishing, rafting, kayaking, camping, and the best skiing in the winter.

There are tons of hiking trails in both parks and there's no better way to experience the Rockies than by strapping on your hiking boots, and climbing your way up the mighty mountains. (But make sure to avoid the cougars!) It's wild and isolated out there, so you'll want to leave your route with someone you trust, and for sure don't go out on your own. The mountains aren't child's play!

Salmonopolis: the fishiest place on the whole west coast

Steveston is a historic village outside Vancouver, located right at the spot where fresh water meets the ocean. This makes it an ideal spot for catching salmon – since most have to pass through this spot during spawning season. Because of this, Steveston became the most important fishing village on the West Coast. By the 1890s, there were 15 salmon canneries there. Salmon and salmon-canning became such a huge part of life in the village that it was often called 'Salmonopolis'. During the summer months, many First Nations, European, Chinese, and Japanese fishermen and cannery workers came to this small village. Many of them stayed, and Steveston quickly began to grow.

Up until World War II, Steveston had one of the largest Japanese-Canadian populations. Many worked on the canning line. But during the war, when Japan attacked Pearl Harbor, panic erupted in British Columbia over Japanese-

Canadians. Many people feared that the Japanese-Canadians in coastal communities would help Japan invade the province. Of course, this fear was unwarranted, but the government caved to public pressure. A sad episode followed where Japanese-owned fishing boats were confiscated and many Japanese-Canadians were sent to internment camps. All ethnic Japanese were ordered out of the area. You can imagine the effect this had on Steveston's population.

Some of the Japanese-Canadians that had been interned or removed from the area did return after the war, however, and today, there still is a large Japanese-Canadian community in Steveston. The village is still a fishing port, although it has also become a popular tourist area and businesses and houses are quickly being built. You can walk along a real fisherman's wharf, get a bite to eat at a restaurant serving freshly caught fish, or visit the Gulf of Georgia Cannery (SEE PaGE 126). Hopefully you don't mind the fishy scent.

cool, yEaH?

The town's name is pronounced 'Steev-ston', not 'Steh-veh-ston'.

Steveston is famous for its fish 'n' chips, so be sure to try some while you're there!

Even though Vancouver is the biggest and busiest city in British Columbia, it's not the province's capital. Victoria is. Like Vancouver, before the Europeans came, Victoria was home to First Nations peoples. In 1843, the Hudson's Bay Company opened a trading post and fort there. It was known as Fort Albert, but was later officially named Fort Victoria, in honour of Queen Victoria.

Around the same time, the Oregon Treaty was being drawn up to establish the International Boundary Line between the United States and British North America (Canada didn't exist yet!). The line would follow the 49th parallel — the area below would be the US, and the area above would be the future Canada. Fort Victoria was at the southern tip of Vancouver Island, which extended south of the 49th parallel. To make sure that the island remained a British

136

territory, the Hudson's Bay Company was given ownership of the entire island, with the condition that it be colonized.

The island became the Crown Colony of Vancouver Island. As colonization proceeded around the fort, Fort Victoria became Victoria. It officially became a city in 1862, 24 years before Vancouver. A few years earlier, in 1858, the Crown Colony of British Columbia was established at Fort Langley (SEE PaGE 122). It didn't make sense to have two separate colonies, so in 1866 the colonies became one. For the next two years, New Westminster was the capital of the new colony.

In 1871, British Columbia became a province of Canada, and Victoria became its capital. As a capital city, Victoria became a government city and for a long time remained the biggest in British Columbia. Because it's so close to the Pacific Ocean, it also became home to a major fishing fleet. However, when the Canadian Pacific Railway was built (ending in Vancouver) Vancouver became the main commercial centre of the province instead.

cool, yEaH?

The city of Victoria has several myths and legends: the Cadborosaurus (or 'Caddy') is a sea serpent that is said to live off the coast. The Mermaid of Active Pass is said to have long blonde hair and was supposedly spotted by ferry passengers sitting on the rocks, eating a salmon.

tRavEl tHRouGH tiME, mEEt cRawly cRittERs, aNd jouRNEy uNdER tHE SEa

If you're really in a rush, it's possible to take a day trip to Victoria from Vancouver, but if you can spare a few days, it's definitely worth taking your time. There's so much to see and do, and the best place to start is at the Inner Harbour and the city's waterfront. Not only is it a great place to sit back, have a soda and people watch, it's also where many attractions are located.

Travel back in time! The **Royal BC Museum** has three permanent galleries: First Peoples, Modern History, and Natural History. Here's your chance to 'discover' the west coast by stepping aboard a replica of Captain George Vancouver's ship HMS Discovery. Take a trip through time and see how British Columbia has changed over millions of years, or experience the First Nations cultures as they were before and after Europeans arrived. There's even an IMAX theatre in the museum.

Want to creep yourself out? The **Victoria Bug Zoo**'s got some of the crawliest creatures in the world. The good news is that you can get a good look at these bugs without worrying about one crawling up your arm… that is, unless you're feeling particularly brave. If you're into that kind of thing, you can handle some real live critters (uh-huh, with your bare hands, but under supervision).

Go underwater without holding your breath! If you're interested in the marine life of British Columbia, there's no better place for you than the **Pacific Undersea Gardens**, located on a large boat. Descend 5 metres (15 feet) below the ocean to see thousands of animals. Watch a live show, or check out the tidal pond where you can touch some of the Pacific's sea life.

Other great places in Victoria include the **Royal London Wax Museum**, the **Maritime Museum of British Columbia**, and **Victoria Butterfly Gardens**. There's plenty to keep you and your family busy for a good, long while.

cool, yEah?

Visit the city's website at www.victoria.ca/visitors where you can download some walking tours that are sure to interest you, including sites from the Gold Rush, or the creepy haunted places in the city.

The Bug Zoo gift shop has some really, umm, interesting things — pet bugs, bug-infused lollipops, or even an insect cookbook! Try it… if you dare!

The promise of a railway to British Columbia was what convinced the colony to join Confederation and form the Canada we have today.

The trains at the park aren't just interesting to look at — many of them still work and are used occasionally for events.

CHOO-CHOO-CHOOSE
WHICH TRAIN TO SEE FIRST

In 1871, the Colony of British Columbia officially joined Canada to become its sixth province. But Canada is a big place, spread over thousands of kilometres, and British Columbia was as far west as possible — a long, long way from Ontario and Québec. The construction of the Canadian Pacific Railway, which began in 1880, was vital to connect B.C. to the rest of Canada.

Building the railway was a huge project. It was also a difficult one, especially in British Columbia where mountains and canyons made work slow and treacherous. Workers were in short supply, and between 1881 and 1884, over 17,000 Chinese men came to British Columbia to help build the railway. Sadly, they were treated unfairly. They were paid less than other workers, were given the worst and most difficult and dangerous jobs, and lived in poor and crowded camps.

Thanks in large part to their hard work, in July 1886, the first train from Montréal arrived in Vancouver. Vancouver was the end (or terminus) of the railway, earning it the nickname Terminal City. It soon became an important port for exporting and importing goods.

Since the railway has been so important in British Columbia's history, it's not surprising that there's a museum that helps preserve and celebrate it. The West Coast Railway Heritage Park looks just like a typical mid-20th century railway facility, with tons of trains and cars, as well as many other railway artifacts for you to see. And if it's all too much to take in on foot, the Miniature Railway's fleet is a quick way to get around the park to see all those locomotives.

it's a whale of a time!

The Pacific Ocean and the Strait of Georgia are full of interesting marine life. But the most impressive sea-dwellers have got to be whales. You won't see any from the city of Vancouver, but there are about 80 of them living off the coast, including orcas, humpbacks, and grey whales. Your whale watching experience will start when you board a boat that will whisk you away into the open waters of the Pacific. Different tours leave from Vancouver and travel south down the Strait of Georgia while others depart from the village of Steveston (SEE PAGE 134). Either way, a unique experience is closer than you think.

There are several types of boats to choose from: open-air zodiacs, covered boats, semi-covered boats, or even large cruise ships. The open-air zodiacs are fast and splashy, and if you don't mind getting a little wet, this one's definitely the way to go. But, be warned. It's a bumpy ride. You might want to take some seasickness pills before you board. Also, make sure to dress warmly — it's usually colder on the ocean than back on land in the city. Your tour operator will supply any gear you need and will point out the marine life along the way. Although the whales are obviously the main attraction, you're also likely to spot dolphins, sea lions, and seals on your adventure.

Some tour operators even offer a once-in-a-lifetime experience: guided kayak tours in the waters around the small islands off Vancouver Island and near Victoria. These tours range from several hours to several days, but are definitely unforgettable. Just remember these important tips: stay at least 100 metres away from the whales, only approach them (or any other marine life) from the side, don't move too quickly, and never feed or swim with the whales.

WHALE WATCHING

cool, yEaH?

Even though orcas are often called killer whales, they aren't whales at all. In fact, they're dolphins! Orcas are also referred to as seawolves or blackfish.

Whales, dolphins, and porpoises are all different and have been found to be descendents of land-living mammals. Their closest living land relative is believed to be the hippopotamus!

cool, yEah?

The Peak 2 Peak Gondola connects the two mountains. It's pretty amazing — a gondola that, at one point, travels 436 m (1,427 feet) over Fitzsimmons Creek. The total ride is 4.4 km (2.73 miles) and takes about 11 minutes.

The Spin Cycle Human Gyroscope is the same as the one used by NASA to give astronauts the feeling of being in space.

Skiing, and so much more!

Vancouver's co-host for the 2010 Winter Olympic and Paralympic Games is the resort town of Whistler. The town is world famous for its ski slopes and winter activities. There are two main mountains — Whistler and Blackcomb. At one time there were separate areas for each mountain, but they came together to form one huge resort called Whistler Blackcomb. Today you don't have to pick one — you have access to it all!

Of course, most people who visit Whistler Blackcomb come for the skiing. But what they soon discover is that there are dozens of other amazing activities to try, and we're not just talking about snowboarding! There are tube rides, snowmobiling, horse-drawn sleigh rides, zip trekking, dog-sledding, snowshoeing, helicopter tours, and more! And that's in the winter alone!

If you've come to Whistler Blackcomb in the summer, you're in for some real fun. This place is a dream for anyone who likes the outdoors and wants to experience adventure after adventure. The resort offers mountain biking, hiking, bear viewing (!), zip trekking, golfing, river rafting, horseback riding, canoeing, fishing... it would take at least a full page to list everything! And you might be surprised to learn that skiing is an option during the summer, too! Plus, the fun doesn't stop there. Whistler Blackcomb has an Adventure Zone just for kids. Here's your chance to try the luge, wall climbing, a bungy trampoline, a human gyroscope, a climbing web, a batting cage, and go-karts.

The Peak 2 Peak Gondola is open all year round. During the winter it takes skiers from one mountain to the other. In the summer, it's a great way to get to all the different activities being offered.

Bard on the Beach
Vanier Park. SkyTrain: Burrard then bus 2 or 22 MacDonald south. Office: 604.737.0625, Box Office: 604.739.0559, www.bardonthebeach.org. Hours: May-Sept: Tues-Sun: Showtimes vary. Check the website for current schedule. Regular Evenings $34, Previews $21.50, 3pm Sat $28.50, 1pm Sat-Sun $21.50, 1pm Tues-Fri $18. Children must be over 6 years old. There is a pre-show and a Q&A after the show on Tues (Jun-Aug). Check the website for registration information for the Young Shakespearean Workshops. Book early as these workshops are very popular. Mon-Fri for two weeks, with a final presentation on Sun.

BC Museum of Mining
Britannia Beach on the Sea to Sky Highway (Highway 99). 604.896.2233, www.bcmuseumofmining.org. Hours: Mar 14-Nov 1: Daily 9am-5pm; Nov & Jan-Mar 13: 9am-4:30pm (Closed for Christmas break). Adults $18.50, Seniors $13.95, Students $13.95, Youth (6-12) $11.95, Children (5 and under) free, Family $55, Self-guided (without train ride) $7.50. Call ahead to confirm tour times. The museum's website has several activities that can be tried at home to get a better understanding of minerals and the mine.

BC Sports Hall of Fame and Museum
BC Place. 777 Pacific Blvd S, Gate A. 604.687.5520, www.bcsportshalloffame.com. Hours: Daily 10am-5pm. Adults $10, Seniors $8, Students $8, Youth (5-17) free, Children (4 and under) free, Family $25. The Hall of Fame has a 'Hero in You' program that helps students and kids learn about themselves and their potential by learning about sports legends.

Beaches
Various locations. Visit www.vancouver.ca/parks/rec/beaches/ for complete information. Locarno Beach, Spanish Banks West Beach, and Sunset Beach are quiet beaches where amplified music isn't allowed. Wreck Beach is a clothing-optional beach near the UBC Campus, advised for those who practise naturism. **English Bay Beach** has concession stands, bathrooms, and kayak rentals. Lifeguards are on duty from Victoria Day to Labour Day. **Kitsilano Beach** has concession stands, a restaurant, bathrooms, heated pool, tennis and basketball courts, and a playground. Lifeguards are on duty from Victoria Day to Labour Day. **Ambleside Beach** has concession stands, bathrooms, playgrounds, pool, pitch and putt golf course, trails, and sailing facilities.

Biking in Vancouver
www.vancouver.ca/cycling. The city produces a pocket-sized map showing the city's bicycle routes. Pick one up at Vancouver public libraries, bike shops, City Hall, or online. Greenways are for non-motorized users only. **Critical Mass**: http://www.bikesexual.org/cm/home.htm. Last Friday of every month. Meet 5pm-5:30pm at Vancouver Art Galley. Critical Mass leaves at 6pm. **BIKE RENTALS: Bayshore Bicycle & Rollerblade Skate Rental:** 745 Denman St. 604.688.BIKE (2453), www.bayshorebikerentals.ca. Hours: Daily: Summer: 9am-9pm; Winter: 9:30am-dusk. **Denman Bike Shop**: 710 Denman St. 604.685.9755, www.denmanbikeshop.com. Hours: Summer: Mon-Thurs 9am-7pm, Fri 9am-6pm, Sat 10am-5pm, Sun 10:30am-4:30pm; Winter: check website. **Spokes Bicycle Rental**: 1798 W Georgia St. 604.688.5141, www.vancouverbikerental.com. Hours: Daily: Summer: 8am-9pm; Winter: check website.

Bill Reid Gallery of Northwest Coast Art
639 Hornby St. SkyTrain: Burrard. 604.682.3455, www.billreidgallery.ca. Hours: Wed-Sun 11am-5pm. Adults $10, Seniors $7, Students $7, Children (5-17) $5, Children (4 and under) free, Family $25. The gallery offers several programs during the year – check the website.

Bloedel Floral Conservatory & Queen Elizabeth Park
Cambie St & West 33rd Ave. SkyTrain: Granville then bus 15 Cambie north. www.vancouver.ca/parks/parks/queenelizabeth/index.htm. **Bloedel**: 604.257.8584. Hours: Sept 1-Apr 30: Daily 10am-8pm; May 1-Aug 31: Mon-Fri 9am-8pm, Sat-Sun 10am-9pm.

Buddhist Temple
International Buddhist Society, 9160 Steveston Hwy, Richmond. SkyTrain: Burrard then bus 403 Three Road south. 604.274.2822, www.buddhisttemple.ca. Hours: Daily 9:30am-5pm. Free (donations accepted). Check out the virtual tour of the temple online. To learn more about Buddhism, visit the BuddhaNet site: www.buddhanet.net/e-learning/basic-guide.htm.

Burnaby Village Museum
6501 Deer Lake Ave, Burnaby. SkyTrain: Metrotown then bus 144 SFU. 604.293.6500, www.burnabyvillagemuseum.ca. Hours: May-Sept: Tues-Sun 11am-4:30pm; Nov-Dec: Tues-Sun times vary. Check website. Adults $12, Seniors $9, Youth (13-18) $9, Children (6-12) $6, Children (5 and under) free. Carousel ride $2. Half price on Tues. Activities for kids: camps, walks, arts & crafts; for adults: blacksmithing, genealogy, walking tours.

Canada Place
999 Canada Place. SkyTrain: Waterfront. 604.689.8232, www.canadaplace.ca/cpc/
Tourist_Information/. Visit the website for a map of the self-guided Promenade Into
History walk, information about events, including Canada Day and Christmas. **Port Metro
Vancouver**: 604.665.9179, www.portmetrovancouver.com. Hours: Mon-Fri 9am-4pm.
Free. Drop-in presentations are on Wed & Fri at 2pm. The centre has plenty of information,
activities, and games for kids. Make sure you ask for the materials. Special events are
held throughout the year. **IMAX**: 604.682.IMAX (4629), www.imax.com/vancouver/. Check
the website for current shows and showtimes. Adults: $12-$14, Seniors $11-$13, Children
(3-12) $11-$13.

Canadian Museum of Flight
Langley Regional Airport – Hangar #3, 5333 216th St, Langley. 604.532.0035, www.
canadianflight.org. Hours: Daily 10am-4pm. Adults $7.55, Seniors $5, Students $5,
Children (under 6) Free, Family $17. Visit the Kids Section of the website to learn about
parts of an airplane. The Millennium Kids Room has hands-on activities and many of the
aircraft can also be touched.

Canoeing, Kayaking and River Rafting
In Vancouver: **Ecomarine Ocean Kayak Centre**: 604.689.7575, www.ecomarine.com.
Several locations: Granville Island, Jericho Beach, English Bay. Outside Vancouver:
Deep Cove Canoe & Kayak: 2156 Banbury Rd, North Vancouver. 604.929.2268, www.
deepcovekayak.com. **Deep Cove Outdoors**: 4310 Gallant Ave, North Vancouver.
604.987.2202, www.deepcoveoutdoors.com. **Canadian Outback**: 604.924.4500, www.
canadianoutback.com. **Chilliwack River Rafting**: 49704 Chilliwack Lake Rd, Chilliwack.
604.824.0334, www.chilliwackriverrafting.com.

Cape Scott Provincial Park
250.956.2260, www.env.gov.bc.ca/bcparks/explore/parkpgs/cape_scott/. Fees apply
and vary based on activity. Check the website for more information. Activities available:
camping, canoeing, fishing, hiking, hunting, swimming, wildlife viewing. Do not leave
anything in the park. Visit the park's website for safety information and bear guidelines.
There are many bears throughout the park.

Capilano River Regional Park
4500 Capilano Park Rd, North Vancouver. SkyTrain: Waterfront then Seabus to Lonsdale
Quay then bus 236 Grouse Mountain. **Important Note**: The canyon can be a very
dangerous place for people of all ages because of the steep and slippery banks that lie
within. Some areas of the canyon are marked with signs and fenced off. Remember that
it's possible for the water level to become dangerously high within a short period of time.
Be aware. It is not possible to safeguard the entire park. Do not leave your parents' side
during your visit.

Capilano Salmon Hatchery
4500 Capilano Park Rd, North Vancouver. SkyTrain: Waterfront then Seabus to Lonsdale
Quay then bus 236 Grouse Mountain. 604.666.1790, www-heb.pac.dfo-mpo.gc.ca/
facilities/capilano/capilano_e.htm. Daily: Nov-Mar 8am-4pm; Apr & Oct 8am-4:45pm; May
& Sept 8am-7pm; Jun-Aug 8am-8pm. Free. A virtual tour of the hatchery is available on
the website, as is a downloadable tour brochure for a self-guided tour of the hatchery.
Please obey all signs.

Capilano Suspension Bridge
3735 Capilano Rd, North Vancouver. SkyTrain: Waterfront then Seabus to Lonsdale Quay
then bus 236 Grouse Mountain. 604.985.7474, www.capbridge.com. Hours: Seasonal:
Daily. Check website. Adults $29.95, Seniors $27.95, Students $23.95, Youth (13-16)
$18.75, Children (6-12) $10, Children (under 6) free. There are different daily activities
– pick up a daily schedule when you enter. Kids can explore the rainforest with Eco the
Bear: an activity book with stickers is available to help kids discover the ecosystem.

Chinatown
SkyTrain: Stadium-Chinatown. www.vancouver-chinatown.com.

Cleveland Dam
Capilano Rd, North Vancouver. SkyTrain: Waterfront then Seabus to Lonsdale Quay then
bus 236 Grouse Mountain. 604.432.6350. The dam is about 1 km north of the Capilano
Salmon Hatchery.

Cypress Mountain
Cypress Provincial Park, Exit 8 off Highway 1, West Vancouver. SkyTrain: Waterfront then
SeaBus to Lonsdale Quay then Cypress Mountain Shuttle (604.419.7669 for more info:

Adults $20, Seniors $15, Youth $15 - roundtrip). 604.926.5612, www.cypressmountain. com. Hours: Seasonal and dependent on activity – check website. Winter downhill lift ticket: Adults $56.19, Seniors $36.19, Youth (13-18) $45.71, Children (6-12) $26.67, Children (5 and under) $7.62. Prices higher during peak periods. Winter cross country trail: Adults $16.98, Seniors $11.32, Youth (13-18) $12.26, Children (6-12) $10.38, Children (5 and under) $4.72. Snowtubing (2 hours) $13.68 ($16.42 during peak period). Snowshoeing: Adults $9.43, Seniors $7.55, Children (6-12) $7.55. Snowshoes extra. Check the website's Weather Centre for current conditions.

Deeley Motorcycle Exhibition
1875 Boundary Rd. SkyTrain: Broadway-Commercial Dr then bus 9 east. 604.293.2221, www.deeleymotorcycleexhibition.ca. Hours: Mon-Fri 10am-5pm, Sat 9:30am-4:30pm, Sun 11am-4:30pm. Admission by donation. Half-hour guided tours are available by request $25. Motorcycles are accessible to visitors but should not be touched – please be careful when closely examining bikes. Running, climbing, and touching are not permitted.

Dr. Sun Yat-Sen Park & Classical Chinese Garden
578 Carrall St, Vancouver. SkyTrain: Stadium-Chinatown. 604.662.3207, www. vancouverchinesegarden.com. **Park**: free. **Classic Chinese Garden**: Daily: May-Jun & Sept 10am-6pm; Jun-Aug 9:30am-7pm; Oct-Apr 10am-4:30pm(closed Mondays Nov-Apr). Adults $10, Seniors $9, Students $8, Children (under 5) Free, Family $24. Self-guided and guided tours are available – check the website for times. The garden offers a series of factsheets about Chinese life and early Chinatown. The set of four extensive factsheets are available for $20.

Ferries and Water Taxis
False Creek Ferries: 604.684.7781, www.granvilleislandferries.bc.ca. Stops: Granville Island, Aquatic Centre, Maritime Museum, Stamp's Landing, Science World, and Yaletown. **Aquabus**: 604.689.5858, www.theaquabus.com. Stops: Downtown (Hornby St), Granville Island, David Lam Park (temporarily closed), Stamp's Landing, Yaletown, Plaza of Nations, Science World. **SeaBus**: 604.953.3333, www.translink.com. Runs every 15-30 minutes between Waterfront station and Londsdale Quay in North Vancouver.

First Nations of British Columbia
Aboriginal Tourism Association of British Columbia. www.aboriginalbc.com.

Fort Langley National Historic Site
23433 Mavis Ave, Fort Langley. SkyTrain: Surrey Central then bus 502 to Langley Centre then Community Shuttle C62 Walnut Grove to Fort Langley. 604.513.4777, www.pc.gc.ca/ lhn-nhs/bc/langley. Hours: Daily: Sept-Jun 10am-5pm; Jun-Sept 9am-8pm. Adults $7.80, Seniors $6.55, Youth $3.90, Family $19.60. A Dual Entry Pass is available for Fort Langley and Gulf of Georgia Cannery: Adults $11.70, Seniors $9.80, Youth $5.80, Family $29.40. Activities and demonstrations run throughout the day and include tours, learning about Chinook Jargon, and life when the fort was used as a trading post.

Gastown
SkyTrain: Waterfront (Cordova Street exit). www.gastown.org. Guided walking tours are available during the summer – check the website for details.

Go-Karting
F440 Racing Challenge: NuLelum Way, (off Highway 17) near Splashdown Park, Tsawwassen. 604.948.2940, www.f440.com. Hours: Apr-Sept: Daily 10am-8pm; Oct-Mar: Daily 10am-dusk. Several types of karts are offered, including regular, kiddie, and double karts. Regular Karts are great for anyone at least 10 years old and 4'8" tall. Double Karts are great for kids under 10 that will ride with an adult. Kiddie Karts are meant for kids ages 8-10 or those that are not yet 4'8" tall. Outdoor track. **Richmond Go Kart Track**: 6631 Sidaway Rd, Richmond. 604.278.6184, www.richmondgokarts.com. Hours: Mar-Oct: Daily noon-sundown. Kids must be at least 10 years old and 4'8" to drive karts on their own. 2-seater karts are available for younger kids. Outdoor track. **TBC Indoor Racing**: 2100 Viceroy Pl, Richmond. 604.232.9196, www.tbcir.ca. Hours: Sun-Wed 10:30am-11pm, Thurs-Sat 10:30am-midnight. Kids must be at least 11 years old and 4'10". Indoor track.

Granville Island
SkyTrain: Waterfront or Granville then bus 50 False Creek south. 604.666.5784, www. granvilleisland.com. **Public Market**: Daily 9am-7pm. **Kids Market**: 604.689.8477, www. kidsmarket.ca. Hours: Daily 10am-6pm. There are many festivals and activities held throughout the year as well as theatre and comedy performances.

Greater Vancouver Zoo
5048 – 264th St, Aldergrove. TransCanada Highway (Highway 1) to exit 73. 604.856.6825,

www.gvzoo.com. Hours: Daily: May-Sept 9am-7pm, Oct-Apr 9am-4pm. Adults $20, Seniors $15, Students $18, Children (4-15) $15, Family $65. Train $5. Parking $4. Reservations (at the entrance) are required for the Safari Miniature Train. Presentations and talks run throughout the day all over the zoo and last 15-20 minutes. To avoid any risks or danger to the animals, please do not touch them.

Grouse Mountain

6400 Nancy Greene Way, North Vancouver. 604.980.9311. SkyTrain: Waterfront then Seabus to Lonsdale Quay then bus 236 Grouse Mountain. Hours: Daily 9am-5pm. Adults: $37.95, Seniors $35.95, Youth $22.95, Children (5-12) $13.95, Children (4 and under) free. Summer Admission includes Skyride, Theatre in the Sky, Refuge for Endangered Wildlife, Lumberjack Show, Birds in Motion, Scenic Chairlift Rides, Mountaintop Eco Walks, and Grouse Grind. Winter Admission includes Skyride, Theatre in the Sky, Refuge for Endangered Wildlife, Snowshoeing, Ice Skating, Sleigh Rides, and Peak of Christmas. Lift tickets and equipment rental extra. The Skyride departs daily every 15 minutes from 9am-10pm. Ziplining: Daily 10am-6pm. $105. Approx 2 hours. Participants must be between 32 kg (70 lbs) and 114 kg (250 lbs). Reservations recommended.

Gulf of Georgia Cannery

Steveston Village, 12138 Fourth Ave, Richmond. SkyTrain: 22nd St then bus 410 Railway south. 604.664.9009, www.pc.gc.ca/georgiacannery. Hours: May-Sept: Mon-Sat 10am-5pm, Sun 11am-5pm; Sept-Oct: Thurs-Mon 10am-5pm (Sun 11am-5pm). Adults $7.80, Seniors $6.55, Youth (6-16) $3.90, Children (under 6) free, Family $19.60. A Dual Entry Pass is available for Fort Langley and Gulf of Georgia Cannery: Adults $11.70, Seniors $9.80, Youth $5.80, Family $29.40. Guided tours are given every hour, on the hour. A short film is shown at 10 minutes and 40 minutes after the hour.

Harbour Cruises

Harbour Cruises and Events: 604.688.7246, www.boatcruises.com. Several tours and destinations available. Check website for details.

Hell's Gate Airtram

43111 TransCanada Highway, Boston Bar. 604.867.9277, www.hellsgateairtram.com. Hours: Daily: May-Sept 10am-5pm; Apr-May & Sept-Oct 10am-4pm. Adults $17, Seniors $15, Students $15, Youth (6-18) $11, Children (5 and under) free, Family $45. Located about 2.5 hours from Vancouver.

H.R. MacMillan Space Centre

Vanier Park, 1100 Chestnut St. SkyTrain: Burrard then bus 2 or 22 MacDonald south. 604.735.5665, www.spacecentre.ca. Hours: Tues-Sun 10am-5pm. Adults $15, Seniors $10.75, Students $10.75, Youth $10.75, Children $10.75, Children (under 5) free, Family $45. Check website for show schedule. Laser shows play on Fri and Sat evenings. $10.75. For a current Vancouver sky chart, visit the website. 5-day Cosmo Camps run in July and August and give participants the chance to perform science experiments and build rockets.

Mount Seymour

1700 Mount Seymour Rd, North Vancouver. 604.986.2261, www.mountseymour.com. Hours: Seasonal – check website. Downhill pass: Adults $44, Seniors $35, Students $37, Youth (13-18) $37, Children (6-12) $22, Children (5 and under) free, Family $124. Equipment rentals extra. Snowtubing (2 hours) $16. Tobogganing $8. Snowshoeing $9. Snowshoes extra. Skiing and snowboarding lessons available.

Museum of Anthropology

University of British Columbia, 6393 NW Marine Dr. SkyTrain: Granville then walk to Howe St then bus 4 or 17 UBC south then Community Shuttle C20. 604.822.3825 or 604.822.5087, www.moa.ubc.ca. Hours: May-Oct: Daily 10am-5pm (Tues to 9pm); Oct-May: Tues-Sun 10am-5pm (Tues to 9pm). Adults $11, Seniors $9, Students $9, Children (6 and under) free, Family $30. Volunteers give free gallery walks twice a day.

Museum of Vancouver

Vanier Park. 1100 Chesnut St. SkyTrain: Burrard then bus 2 or 22 MacDonald south. 604.736.4431, www.museumofvancouver.ca. Hours: Sept-Jun: Tues-Sun 10am-5pm (Thurs to 8pm); Jul-Aug: Daily 10am-5pm (Thurs to 8pm). Adults $11, Seniors $9, Students $9, Youth (5-17) $7, Children (under 5) free, Family $32. On weekends, the museum offers a variety of workshops and activities, as well as a self-guided scavenger hunt. Check the website for current events.

Olympic Information

www.vancouver2010.com.

Pacific Rim National Park
2185 Ocean Terrace Rd, Ucluelet. 250.726.3500, www.pc.gc.ca/pn-np/bc/pacificrim. Adults $9.80, Seniors $8.30, Youth $4.90, Family $19.60. Camping extra. Activities include boating, camping, bird watching, fishing, whale, seal and sea lion watching. Check the website for more information, safety guidelines, maps (including the West Coast Trail map).

Playland & the Pacific National Exhibition
Hastings Park, 2901 East Hastings St. SkyTrain: Renfrew then bus 16 Arbutus. 604.253.2311, www.pne.ca. Playland: Check website for dates and hours. One-Day pass $29.95, Jr One-Day pass $19.95. Seniors free. PNE: last three weeks of the summer, ending on Labour Day.

Regional Parks
www.metrovancouver.org/services/parks_lscr/regionalparks. Always check the website for updates on the conditions at the various parks. The website includes any advisories that may be important, including fires.

Robson Square
SkyTrain: Granville.

Rocky Mountains
Banff National Park: 224 Banff Ave (Information Centre), Banff, Alberta. 403.762.1550, www.pc.gc.ca/pn-np/ab/banff. Hours: Seasonal - check website. Adults $9.80, Seniors $8.30, Youth $4.90, Family $19.60. Camping and fishing extra. **Jasper National Park**: 500 Connaught Dr (Information Centre), Jasper, Alberta. 780.852.6176, www.pc.gc.ca/pn-np/ab/jasper. Hours: Seasonal - check website. Adults $9.80, Seniors $8.30, Youth $4.90, Family $19.60. Camping and fishing extra. Jasper and Banff are about 10 hours from Vancouver. For hiking, camping, climbing, and skiing, a wilderness pass and reservations may be required. A national parks permit is required to travel on the Icefields Parkway. Visit the website and review the safety information, which includes: what to do if approached by a wild animal, rock and ice, drinking water, and insects.

Science World
1455 Quebec St. SkyTrain: Main Street-Science World. 604.443.7443, www.scienceworld. ca. Hours: Daily 10am-6pm. Adults $19.75, Seniors $16.25, Students $16.25, Youth $16.25, Children (4-12) $13.75, Family $71.50. Ultimate Experience (includes one OMNIMAX film): Adults $24.75, Seniors $21.25, Students $21.25, Youth $21.25, Children (4-12) $18.75. OMNIMAX only $10. Science World offers changing weekend activities and programs as well as birthday parties and overnight and summer camps. The website has plenty of activities that can be done at home. The Feature Gallery exhibit changes several times a year. There are plenty of hands-on activities and staffers are available to answer questions.

Seaplane Tours
Harbour Air Seaplanes: 604.274.1277, www.harbourair.com. **Westcoast Air**: 604.606.6888, www.westcoastair.com. Both companies offer several tours and destinations. Check their websites for details.

Sports Teams
Visit the teams' websites for team information, schedule, and tickets. **BC Lions** www.bclions.com; **Vancouver Canucks** canucks.nhl.com; **Vancouver Whitecaps FC** www.whitecapsfc.com; **Western Lacrosse Association** www.theboxrocks.com.

Stanley Park
SkyTrain: Burrard then bus 19 Stanley Park west. www.vancouver.ca/parks/parks/stanley. Information Booth: 604.681.6728. **Children's Farmyard & Miniature Railway**: Hours: Seasonal – check website. Adults $6, Seniors $4.25, Youth $4.25, Children (2-12) $3. During the summer, a shuttle bus travels around the park and makes 15 stops. Adults $2, Children (2-11) $1 for all day pass. **Horse-Drawn Tours**: 604.681.5115, www.stanleypark.com. Hours: Mar-Oct: Seasonal. Adults $26.99, Seniors $24.99, Students $24.99, Children (3-12) $14.99. **Stanley Park Ecology Society** offers a variety of public programs, including park walks, bird watching, and overnight activities. **Pitch & Putt**: 604.681.8847. Hours: Summer 7:30am-dusk; Winter 9am-dusk (Putting Green Jul-Sept: 12noon-7:30pm). Green Fees: Adults $12.50, Seniors $8.85, Youth $8.85. Putting Green: Adults $4, Seniors $2.75, Youth $2.75, Children $2. Clubs and caddy rental extra.

Steveston Village
SkyTrain: 22nd St then bus 410 Railway. www.stevestonvillage.com.

UBC Botanical Garden & Nitobe Memorial Garden
University of British Columbia. SkyTrain: Granville then walk to Howe St then bus 4 or 17 UBC south then Community Shuttle C20. **UBC Botanical Garden**: 6804 SW Marine Dr.

604.822.9666, www.ubcbotanicalgarden.org. Hours: Mon-Fri 9am-5pm, Sat-Sun 9:30am-5:30pm. Adults $8, Seniors $6, Students $6, Youth (13-17) $6, Children (12 and under) free, Family $12. Audioguide $2. **Greenheart Canopy Walkway**: Hours: Daily each hour starting at 10am (Sept to Jun: Wed tours start at 12noon). Adults $20, Seniors $16, Students $16, Youth (13-17) $14, Children (5-12) $6 (price includes admission to UBC Botanical Garden). A self-guided tour for kids is available. **Nitobe Memorial Garden**: 604.822.9666, www.nitobe.org. Hours: Seasonal – check website. Adults $6, Seniors $5, Students $3, Youth (13-17) $2, Children (12 and under) free, Family $9. During the summer, visitors can witness the preparation of tea during a tea ceremony. Reservations are recommended (604.939.7749).

Vancouver Aquarium
Stanley Park, 845 Avison Way. 604.659.3521, www.vanaqua.org. Hours: Daily 9:30am-7pm. Adults $28, Seniors $22, Youth (13-18) $22, Children (4-12) $18, Children (3 and under) free. Animal Encounters book up fast so contact the aquarium to reserve early (604.659.3552). Children must be over the age of 8, and if under 13, must be accompanied by an adult. Events and activities offered include sleepovers, camps, and clubs. Some programs in French are available. Visit the website to view the Beluga and Otter Cams or Kids' Zone, an interactive experience focusing on ocean science.

Vancouver Art Gallery
750 Hornby St. SkyTrain: Granville. 604.662.4719, www.vanartgallery.bc.ca. Hours: Daily 10am-5:30pm (Tues & Thurs to 9pm). Adults $20.50, Seniors $16, Students $15, Children (5-12) $7, Children (4 and under) free, Family $50. Art Agents: Sat 12noon-4pm; Art Tracks: Sat 2pm; The Making Place: 2nd and 4th Sun, 12noon-4pm. Cameras, backpacks, food, drinks, large bags, and umbrellas are not allowed in the galleries. A coatcheck is available. Cameras are allowed in The Making Place only. Part of the gallery's collection is viewable online at: projects.vanartgallery.bc.ca/publications/75years/.

Vancouver Folk Music Festival
Jericho Beach Park. Bus 4. 604.602.9798, www.thefestival.bc.ca. Hours: three days in July: gates open Fri 4pm & Sat-Sun 10am. Weekend Pass: Adults $165, Seniors $73, Students $95, Youth (13-18) $73, Children (12 and under) free with adult.

Vancouver International Children's Festival
Vanier Park. SkyTrain: Burrard then bus 2 or 22 MacDonald south. 604.708.5655, www.childrensfestival.ca. Hours: One week in May – check website for schedule of events. Site Admission $10. Show tickets $16 (includes site admission). Variety show tickets: Adults $20, Youth $18. Tickets can be purchased at www.ticketmaster.ca, by phone (604.280.3311) or at the on-site box office.

Vancouver Lookout
555 West Hastings St. SkyTrain: Waterfront. 604.689.0421, www.vancouverlookout.com. Hours: Daily: May-Oct 8:30am-10:30pm; Oct-Apr 9am-9pm. Adults $13, Seniors $11, Students $9, Youth (13-18) $9, Children (6-12) $6, Children (5 and under) free. Guided tours are available. The website has a Kids section with information, colouring sheets, and a Building Quiz. Tickets are for the day – you can come and go as much as you like. **Top of Vancouver Revolving Restaurant** 604.669.2220, www.topofvancouver.com.

Vancouver Maritime Museum
Vanier Park, 1905 Ogden Ave. SkyTrain: Burrard then bus 2 or 22 MacDonald south. 604.257.8300, www.vancouvermaritimemuseum.com. Hours: May-Sept: Daily 10am-5pm; Sept-May: Tues-Sat 10am-5pm, Sun 12noon-5pm. Adults $10, Seniors $7.50, Youth (6-18) $7.50, Children (5 and under) free. The museum's website has virtual tours of the St Roch and the Ben Franklin. The Children's Maritime Discovery Centre offers hands-on activities.

Vancouver Police Museum
240 East Cordova St. SkyTrain: Granville then bus 4 Powell. 604.665.3346, www.vancouverpolicemuseum.ca. Hours: Mon-Sat 9am-5pm. Adults $7, Seniors $5, Students $5, Children (under 6) free, Family $20. Tours run during the summer on Wednesdays, Fridays, and Saturdays. During certain times of the year, families can drop in and learn all about forensic science hands-on: take fingerprints, examine bullets and analyze evidence!

Vancouver Public Library
350 West Georgia St. SkyTrain: Granville or Stadium-Chinatown. 604.331.3603, www.vpl.ca/branches/details/central_library and www.vpl.ca/kids. Hours: Mon-Thurs 10am-9pm, Fri-Sat 10am-6pm, Sun 12noon-5pm.

VanDusen Botanical Garden
5251 Oak St. SkyTrain: Granville then bus 17 Oak west. 604.878.9274, www.

vandusengarden.org. Seasonal: Daily: Nov-Feb 10am-4pm; Mar & Oct 10am-5pm; Apr 10am-6pm; May 10am-8pm; Jun-Aug 10am-9pm; Sept 10am-7pm; Apr-Sept: Adult $8.85, Senior $6.50, Youth (13-18) $6.50, Child (6-12) $4.70, Child (under 6) free, Family $20.30. Oct-Mar: Adult $6.50, Senior $4.70, Youth (13-18) $4.70, Child (6-12) $3.40, Child (under 6) free, Family $13.50. A map shows various walking routes, and a self-guided tour for children is available. The Garden offers camps and programs during the summer for kids and families. Check out the website for more information. For more information about the Wollemi Pine, check out www.wollemipine.com.

Victoria

Tourism Victoria: www.tourismvictoria.com. City of Victoria: www.victoria.ca/visitors. **Royal BC Museum**: 675 Belleville St, Victoria. 250.356.RBCM (7226), www.royalbcmuseum. bc.ca. Hours: Daily 9am-5pm. Adults $27.50, Seniors $18.50, Students $18.50, Youth (6-18) $18.50, Children (3-5) free, Family $73.50. **Victoria Bug Zoo**: 631 Courtney St, Victoria. 250.384.2847, www.bugzoo.bc.ca. Hours: Mon-Sat 10am-6pm, Sun 11am-6pm. Adults $8, Seniors $7, Youth (13-19) $6, Children (3-12) $5. **Pacific Undersea Gardens**: 490 Belleville St, Victoria. 250.382.5717, www.pacificunderseagardens.com. Hours: Daily: Sept-Apr 10am-5pm; May-Jun 10am-5pm (Thurs-Sun to 7:30pm); Jul-Sept 9am-8pm. Adults $9.75, Seniors $8.75, Youth (12-17) $7.75, Children (5-11) $5.75, Children (under 5) free. **Royal London Wax Museum**: 470 Belleville St, Victoria. 250.388.4461, www.waxmuseum.bc.ca. Hours: Daily 9am-9pm. Adults $12, Seniors $11, Students $9, Children $6. **Maritime Museum of British Columbia**: 28 Bastion Square, Victoria. 250.385.4222, www.mmbc.bc.ca. Hours: Opens daily 9:30am. Adults $10, Seniors $8, Students $8, Children (6-11) $5, Family $25. **Victoria Butterfly Gardens**: 1461 Benvenuto Ave, Brentwood Bay. 250.652.3822, www. butterflygardens.com. Hours: Daily: Feb 10am-4pm; Mar-Apr & Sept-Oct 9:30am-4:30pm; May-Aug 9am-5pm, Nov-Dec 9am-4pm. Adults $12, Seniors $11, Students $11, Children (3-12) $6.50.

Water Parks & Pools

Bridal Falls Waterpark: 53790 Popkum Rd S, Rosedale. 604.794.7455, www. bridalfallswaterpark.com. Hours: Seasonal – check website. $17. Lifejackets, lockers, mini golf extra. About 1.5 hours from Vancouver. **Cultus Lake Waterpark**: 4150 Columbia Valley Highway, Cultus Lake. 604.858.7241, www.cultus.com. Hours: Seasonal – check website. Full day pass $24.76, Under 48" tall $17.14, Seniors $17.14. About 1.5 hours from Vancouver. **Granville Island Waterpark**: Granville Island. www.granvilleisland.com. Hours: May-Sept: Daily 10am-6pm. Free. **Minoru Aquatic Centre**: 7560 Minoru Gate, Richmond. 604.718.8020, www.richmond.ca/parksrec/pools/minoru.htm. **Newton Wave Pool**: 13730 – 72nd Ave, Surrey. 604.501.5540, www.surrey.ca. **Splashdown Park**: 4799 Nulelum Way, Tsawwassen. 604.943.2251, www.splashdownpark.ca. Hours: Seasonal – check website. Full day pass $20.95, Under 48" tall $14.95, Family $72.95. **Surrey Sport and Leisure Complex**: 16555 Fraser Highway, Surrey. 604.501.5950, www.surrey.ca. **Watermania**: 14300 Entertainment Blvd, Richmond. 604.448.5353, www.richmond.ca/parksrec/pools/ watermania.htm.

West Coast First Nations

Aboriginal Tourism Association of British Columbia. www.aboriginalbc.com.

West Coast Railway Heritage Park

39645 Government Rd, Squamish. 604.898.9336, www.wcra.org. Hours: Daily 10am-5pm. Adults $10, Seniors $8.50, Students $8.50, Family $32.

Whale Watching

Many companies offer whale watching tours and adventures. May to October are the best times for whale watching. **Prince of Whales** www.princeofwhales.com; **Steveston Seabreeze Adventures** www.seabreezeadventures.ca; **Vancouver Whale Watch** www. vancouverwhalewatch.com; **Wild Whales Vancouver** www.whalesvancouver.ca. **Kayaking Adventures**: Tourism Information: www.hellobc.com/whalewatching. **Quadra Island Kayaks** www.quadraislandkayaks.com/index.html; **Spirit of the West** www.kayakingtours.com; **Sea Kayaking British Columbia** www.outforadventure.com; **Coastal Spirits Expeditions** www. kayakbritishcolumbia.com; **Pacific Northwest Expeditions** www.seakayakbc.com.

Whistler-Blackcomb

4545 Blackcomb Way, Whistler. 604.932.3434, www.whistlerblackcomb.com. Hours: Seasonal and dependent on activity – check website. Skiing and snowboarding lessons are available for skiers of all ages and experience, starting from 3 years old. About 2 hours from Vancouver, by car along the Sea to Sky Highway (Highway 99). To get to Whistler by train, try the Whistler Mountaineer: 604.606.8460, www.whistlermountaineer.com.

REComMENdEd apaRtmENt SERvicEs

Renting an apartment in Vancouver, especially when you are travelling with kids, is a great option that provides added freedom, character, and space for less money. There are many options, with apartments available in every size and price range, all over the Greater Vancouver Area. Dream Vacation Rental is a Vancouver-based company that offers condos and townhouses. Rentals include internet, cable TV, full kitchen, and washer & dryer. Visit their website: **www.dreamvacationrent.com**

chILd–FRiENdly HoTEl pick

PACIFIC PALISADES HOTEL * * * * *1277 Robson St., Vancouver, B.C. V6E 1C4. Tel 604.688.0461 or 800.663.1815 Fax 604.688.4374 E-mail reservations@pacificpalisadeshotel.com. www.pacificpalisadeshotel.com*

The Pacific Palisades Hotel is a great choice for families and kids. Located in downtown Vancouver on Robson Street, this bright and colourful hotel is just a short walk from many of the city's highlights, including the waterfront and Seawall. The hotel offers a special kids' package which includes a travel activity bag upon check-in, bedtime snacks of milk and cookies, and Continental breakfast for four at the ZIN Restaurant & Lounge.

Babysitting services are available and the hotel can provide a list of kid-friendly restaurants and activities in the area. There is a complimentary wine reception every night (with fresh juice for kids). Most rooms are suites, each with a kitchenette and internet access. A swimming pool and spa services, including children's spa services are also available. The relaxed atmosphere and friendly and helpful staff make the Pacific Palisades Hotel a top pick. Vancouver's 'eco-friendly' hotel is also pet-friendly, so feel free to bring along your four-legged family members, too!

Photograph credits and copyrights (clockwise from top left):

Cover Art: Tapan Gandhi (logo); Ran Kim (drawing); Kim Sokol (stamp); A.J. Palmer (font).
Characters: Tapan Gandhi. **All stamps:** Kim Sokol.

Front cover endpaper: courtesy Tourism Vancouver/The Greater Vancouver Visitors and Convention Bureau (cropped). 1: stamp Kim Sokol; base photo HighInBC /wc/cc-by-sa-2.5 (cropped). 7: DavidArthur /wc/cc-by-sa-3.0 (edited). 8: /w/pd. 9: courtesy City of Vancouver. 10: /w/pd. 11-12: all courtesy City of Vancouver. 13: sw/jj. 14-15: Thom Quine /wc/cc-by-2.0 (cropped). 16-17: Matthew Field /wc/cc-by-sa-3.0 (cropped). 19: courtesy Capilano Suspension Bridge (CSB); courtesy CSB; courtesy CSB; sw/jj; courtesy CSB. 20-21: all sw/jj. 22: all sw/jj. 24: sw/jj; /w/pd; Zotium /wc/cc-by-sa-3.0. 27: /w/pd; /w/pd; sw/jj. 28: Reinhard Kraasch /wc/cc-by-sa-3.0; all others sw/jj. 31: courtesy BC Sports Hall of Fame; sw/jj. 32-33: Trifon Marchovski/Bill Reid Gallery of Northwest Coast Art; Kenji Nagai/Bill Reid Gallery of Northwest Coast Art. 34: all sw/jj. 36: sw/jj; sw/jj; sw/jj; Grapeman /wc/cc-by-sa-3.0; courtesy Canada Place. 37: sw/jj. 39: Arnold C /wc; sw/jj; Arnold C /wc (cropped). 40: sw/jj. 42: Arnold C /wc; sw/jj. 43: sw/jj. 45: all courtesy Deeley Motorcycle Exhibition. 46: sw/jj; /wc/pd; sw/jj; sw/jj; /wc/pd. 49: Ken Medoro. 51: all courtesy Grouse Mountain. 52: all courtesy H.R. MacMillan Space Centre. 53: NASA /pd; all others sw/jj. 54: all sw/jj. 57: all sw/jj. 59: sw/jj. 61: PNE Photographer/PNE; ThePointblank /wc/cc-by-sa-3.0; PNE Photographer/PNE. 62: TUBS /wc/cc-by-sa-3.0; all others Philippe Giabbanelli /wc/cc-by-3.0. 65: all sw/jj. 66: all sw/jj. 69: /wc/pd. 71: sw/jj; Daniel Mosquin/UBC Botanical Garden; sw/jj. 72: Noel Hendrickson/Vancouver Aquarium; Margaret Butschler/Vancouver Aquarium; Hamid Attie/Vancouver Aquarium. 74: all sw/jj. 77: /wc/pd; courtesy Vancouver Lookout. 79: all sw/jj. 80-81: all sw/jj. 82-83: all sw/jj. 85: sw/jj; N. Wong/VanDusen Botanical Garden (cropped); Stan Shebs /wc/cc-by-sa-3.0. 87: sw/jj; Booyabazooka /wc/cc-by-sa-3.0; courtesy Bard on the Beach. 88: sw/jj. 89: Jeff W Brooktree /f/cc-by-sa-2.0; all other sw/jj. 90: sw/jj. 91: Duncan Rawlinson /wc/cc-by-2.0; Tavis Ford /wc/cc-by-2.0. 92-93: all sw/jj. 95: /wc/pd. 97: sw/jj. 99: all sw/jj. 100: Andrew W (Tawker) /wc/cc-by-2.5. 101: sw/jj. 102: Christian Muise /wc/cc-by-sa-2.0. 103: Joe Perez/Vancouver Folk Music Festival. 104: courtesy Vancouver International Children's Festival. 107: all courtesy Bridal Falls Water Park. 109: all courtesy BC Museum of Mining. 110: all sw/jj. 113: all courtesy Burnaby Village Museum. 114-115: all sw/jj. 118-119: all Joffrey Koeman/Cypress Mountain (cropped). 123: sw/jj; Napa /wc/cc-by-sa-3.0; sw/jj; Napa /wc/cc-by-sa-3.0; sw/jj. 124: courtesy Greater Vancouver Zoo (GVZ); courtesy GVZ; sw/jj. 125: Zoologic font Daniel Zadorozny. 127: sw/jj. 129: Jonathan Rodgers /w/cc-by-sa-2.5; courtesy Hell's Gate Airtram (HGA); courtesy HGA; Jonathan Rodgers /w/cc-by-sa-2.5. 130: Burtonpe /w/cc-by-sa-2.5. 132-133: Tobias Alt /w/cc-by-sa-3.0. 134-135: all sw/jj. 138: courtesy Royal BC Museum. 143: Zoran Kovacevic /w/cc-by-sa-2.5; Jim Harper /w/cc-by-sa-1.0 (cropped). 144: Thom Quine /wc/cc-by-2.0 (cropped); Mogodore /wc/cc-by-sa-3.0 (cropped); /wc/pd. 153: Andrew Raun /wc/cc-by-sa-2.0; all others Pacific Palisades Hotel; Jordi character Mike Hiscott. 154-155: sw/jj. **Back cover end paper:** courtesy Tourism Vancouver/The Greater Vancouver Visitors and Convention Bureau (cropped).

Acronyms: (cc-by-0.0) Creative Commons Attribution version #; **(cc-by-sa-0.0)** Creative Commons Attribution ShareAlike version #; **(f)** Flickr; **(jj)** Junior Jetsetters; **(pd)** Public Domain; **(sw)** Slawko Waschuk; **(w)** Wikipedia/Wikimedia; **(wc)** Wikimedia Commons.

Every effort has been made to accurately credit all photos. If you believe an error has been made, please contact us and we will correct it in future editions.

METRo vaNCouvER

A

"Sea to Sky" Highway & Pemberton

99

LIONS BAY

Cypress Provincial Park

B.C. Ferries Terminal

HORSESHOE BAY

Lighthouse Park

WEST VANCOUVER

MARINE DR

Lynn Headwaters Regional Park

Lower Seymour Conservation Reserve

Grouse Mountain

Capilano Suspension Bridge

NORTH VANCOUVER

Lynn Canyon Park

Lynn Valley Park

Mount Seymour Provincial Park

Northlands Golf Course

MT. SEYMOUR PKWY

DOLLARTON HWY

Maplewood Farm

DEE COV

B

LONSDALE AVE.

LYNN VALLEY RD.

TAYLOR WAY

Cliff Taylor Blvd

To Grouse Mtn.

Marine Dr

Marine Dr

Marine Dr

Welch St.

Lions Gate Bridge

Marine Dr

Stanley Park

English Bay

Park & Tilford Garden & Shops

Hastings Racecourse

BURRARD INLET

Burrard Inlet

C

Strait of Georgia

UBC Museum of Anthropology

POINT GREY

University of British Columbia

University Golf Club

UBC Botanical Gardens

DOWNTOWN

HASTINGS

4TH AVE.

ALMA ST.

10TH

BROADWAY

12TH AVE.

ARBUTUS

VanDusen Botanical Gardens

GRANVILLE ST.

DUNBAR ST.

S.W. MARINE DR.

McCleery Golf Course

OAK ST.

CAMBIE ST.

Queen Elizabeth Park

41 AVE.

49 AVE.

Langara Golf Course

VANCOUVER

Bloedel Floral Conservatory

COMMERCIAL DR

1ST AVE.

P.N.E. / Playland

Fraserview Golf Course

KNIGHT ST.

North Arm Fraser River

MARINE DR.

99A

BOUNDARY RD.

WILLINGDON

LOUGHEED

BU

BU

Burnaby Museum

Deer Lake

12TH

CAN

NEW WESTMIN

D

Vancouver International Airport

RICHMOND FWY.

Maytair Lakes Golf Course

WESTMINSTER HWY.

Richmond Go-Kart Track

RICHMOND

NO. 1 RD.

GILBERT RD.

NO. 3 RD.

BRIDGEPORT RD.

91

99

South Arm Fraser River

RIVER RD.

ALEX FRASER BRIDGE

NEW WESTMIN

E

STEVESTON

STEVESTON HWY.

Gulf of Georgia National Historic Site of Canada

International Buddhist Temple

WESTHAM IS. RD.

18TH AVE.

46A ST.

72ND ST.

10

LADNER TRUNK RD.

LADNER

Boundary Bay Airport

17

DELTA

F

28TH AVE.

12TH AVE.

NO. RD.

TSAWWASSEN

Boundary Bay

G

Deltaport

1ST AVE.

B.C. Ferries Terminal To Victoria and Gulf Islands

Point Roberts Border Crossing

BRITISH CO

WASHIN

1   **2**   **3**   **4**